T0016383

# THE MINI ROUGH GUIDE TO
# JERSEY

ROUGH
GUIDES

# YOUR TAILOR-MADE TRIP
## STARTS HERE

**Tailor-made trips and unique adventures crafted by local experts**

Rough Guides has been inspiring travellers for more than 35 years. Leave it to our local experts to create your perfect itinerary and book it at local rates.

Don't follow the crowd – find your own path.

## HOW ROUGHGUIDES.COM/TRIPS WORKS

**STEP 1** Pick your dream destination, tell us what you want and submit an enquiry.

**STEP 2** Fill in a short form to tell your local expert about your dream trip and preferences.

**STEP 3** Our local expert will craft your tailor-made itinerary. You'll be able to tweak and refine it until you're completely satisfied.

**STEP 4** Book online with ease, pack your bags and enjoy the trip! Our local expert will be on hand 24/7 while you're on the road.

# PLAN AND BOOK YOUR TRIP AT
# ROUGHGUIDES.COM/TRIPS

# HOW TO DOWNLOAD YOUR FREE EBOOK

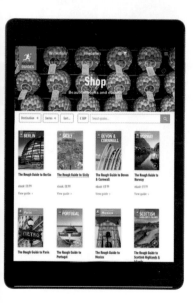

1. Visit **www.roughguides. com/free-ebook** or scan the **QR code** below

2. Enter the code **jersey632**

3. Follow the simple step-by-step instructions

For troubleshooting contact: mail@roughguides.com

# **10** THINGS NOT TO MISS

**1**

**2**

**3**

**4**

ROZEL
← 1½ MILES
BOULEY BAY
½ MILE →

**6**

**5**

**7**

1. **MARITIME MUSEUM**
   A first-rate museum that brings to life Jersey's former seafaring role, ideal for adults and children. See page 34.

2. **SAMARÈS MANOR**
   A medieval manor renowned for its unique gardens and extensive range of plants. See page 45.

3. **MONT ORGUEIL CASTLE**
   The stately symbol of the island dominates Gorey Harbour from its rocky promontory. See page 77.

4. **ELIZABETH CASTLE**
   On guard at the great Tudor stronghold, which was once occupied by Sir Walter Raleigh. See page 36.

5. **JERSEY WAR TUNNELS**
   An extraordinary complex of bomb-proof barracks constructed by the Germans. See page 38.

6. **NORTH COAST FOOTPATH**
   The most exhilarating walk on the island, linking a chain of pretty bays such as Grève de Lecq. See pages 62 and 90.

7. **LA HOUGUE BIE**
   One of the largest and best-preserved Neolithic passage graves in Europe. See page 42.

8. **BEAUPORT BEACH**
   The islanders' favourite beach in a beautiful unspoilt bay. See page 54.

9. **JERSEY MUSEUM AND ART GALLERY**
   Provides an excellent introduction to the history and culture of the island. See page 28.

10. **JERSEY ZOO**
    Renowned zoo established by Gerald Durrell in 1959 for the protection of endangered species. See page 69.

# A PERFECT DAY

### 9.00am

**Breakfast.** Indulge in a buffet breakfast in the Harbour Room of the Pomme d'Or Hotel in the heart of St Helier (Liberation Square; breakfast Mon–Sun from 7am–10am, lunch Sun noon–2pm) and enjoy views of the yacht marina across the square.

### 10.00am

**Picture-postcard harbour.** Head out east from St Helier to Gorey, where a pretty harbour sits below the great medieval stronghold of Mont Orgueil. Climb the ramparts for magnificent views, stroll around the harbour and stop for coffee on the quayside.

### 12 noon

**Heading north.** Explore at least a section of the majestic north coast, with its towering cliffs and perfect little fishing ports. Head north from Gorey via the B30 and B46, pass Gerald Durrell's famous Jersey Zoo , then dip down to quaint Bonne Nuit Bay, its tiny harbour sheltered by a single stone jetty.

### 12.45pm

**Cliff walk.** Pick up the cliff footpath eastwards in the direction of Bouley Bay to see some of the North Coast's most spectacular scenery. For lunch try the seafood, crab sandwiches or Thai specials at Bonne Nuit's café, overlooking the pretty bay.

### 2.00pm

**St Aubin.** Return to the south coast via the scenic Waterworks Valley and head east for St Aubin. Explore the

# IN **JERSEY**

port, browse in the Harbour Gallery arts and crafts centre, then head on west for St Brelade's Bay.

### 3.30pm

**Afternoon relaxation.** Relax on the beach here, take a dip or try your hand at blokarting or paddleboarding. If a quiet beach is more your scene, head a short distance west for the beautiful little bay of Beauport, reached down a bracken-covered cliff.

### 6.00pm

**Corbière.** It's only a short hop to Corbière Lighthouse, Jersey's most dramatic landmark. Watch the sun sink into the Atlantic.

### 7.00pm

**Dinner options.** Then enjoy gourmet fare at the Ocean Restaurant, Atlantic Hotel, with sublime views over St Ouen's Bay (book in advance). Cheaper options are pub grub with bay views at La Pulente in St Ouen's Bay, or the seafood cafés along St Brelade's Bay.

### 10.00pm

**On the town.** Back in St Helier spend a relaxing evening at the Royal Yacht Hotel, Weighbridge, right in the centre. Choose from bubbles in the P.O.S.H Bar or a nice quiet pint in the snug The Peirson. Alternatively just go with the flow in The Drift, a live music venue.

# CONTENTS

## HIGHLIGHTS

## A NOTE TO READERS

At Rough Guides, we always strive to bring you the most up-to-date information. This book was produced during a period of continuing uncertainty caused by the Covid-19 pandemic, so please note that content is more subject to change than usual. We recommend checking the latest restrictions and official guidance.

# OVERVIEW

Lying in the Bay of Mont St Michel, just 14 miles (22km) from the Normandy coast, Jersey has a distinct Gallic twist. The moment you arrive you have a sense of being abroad. Airport and harbour greet you with *Seyiz les beinv'nus a Jèrri* (Welcome to Jersey) in the French Norman patois, street and place names are still written in French, islanders are known as *crapauds* (toads) and every restaurant has a *plateau de fruits de mer*. Yet Jersey feels reassuringly familiar to UK visitors. Although it's not truly British, it has been linked with the British Crown for over 900 years, the official language is English, you drive on the left and cash machines dispense sterling. In other words, Jersey has the best of both worlds.

Tilting southwards, the island basks in the sun like a vast solar panel. The coastline offers a remarkable range of scenery from the vertiginous craggy cliffs of the north, to the Atlantic rollers of the windswept west, and the sweeping flat sands of the south. Along with its French flavour, the island offers all the ingredients of a traditional British seaside holiday: sandy beaches, crab-filled rock pools, big tides for beachcombing, picturesque fishing ports and ample family attractions. The sands of Jersey are washed by clear blue seas and the island has one of the largest tidal movements in the world. Twice a day waters retreat to reveal large expanses of golden sand or lunar-like seascapes, pierced with rocks and reefs. At low tide the island almost doubles in size – then the sea comes galloping in.

In the unlikely event that you tire of the coast, Jersey packs in plenty of other

### A big name

Jersey may be a tiny speck on the map but the island has given its name to a breed of cow, a potato, a pullover, a lily, and a state in America.

attractions. Its tempestuous history has left a mark in monuments ranging from Neolithic tombs to castles, coastal towers and wartime tunnels and bunkers. With walkers and cyclists in mind, Jersey has developed a network of 'Green Lanes', where traffic is restricted to 15 mph (24kmph). Even on main roads the pace is slow, with a maximum speed limit of 40mph (64kmph). Inland Jersey is lush and pretty with wooded valleys, leafy lanes and pastures of doe-eyed cows.

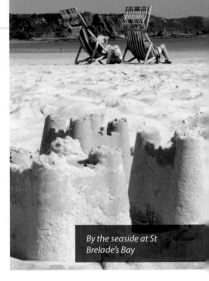

By the seaside at St Brelade's Bay

But Jersey is no sleepy backwater. St Helier is a buzzing capital and haven of high finance; former grand hotels have been given multimillion facelifts, with swish spas added; forts and follies have been converted to stylish self-catering complexes; and beach resorts have seen a surge of adrenalin-fuelled sports. On the culinary scene Jersey has made quite a name for itself, with restaurants producing exceptional, freshly caught seafood. Walking and cycling may be encouraged, but Jersey has one of the highest car ownership and user rates in the world.

## 'PECULIAR OF THE CROWN'

Neither wholly French nor English, Jersey has a quirky history and some unique, quasi-feudal customs. The Channel Islands are termed a 'Peculiar of the Crown', pledging allegiance directly to the English Crown, not to the parliament of the UK. As the last remaining territories of the dukes of Normandy, they toast the Queen of England as 'Our Duke of Normandy'. They are not full members of the EU – though when Britain joined (the EEC) in 1973, the Channel Islands were granted special privileges. Jersey has its own government, legal system and even its own non-uniformed honorary police force who have operated since Norman times and who alone can formally charge a suspect. The island prints its own currency and still has a £1 note (which went out of circulation in the rest of Britain in the early 1980s); it also issues its own stamps.

## SIZE AND CLIMATE

Jersey may be the largest of the Channel Islands, but it is still a tiny island, measuring 9 miles (14km) long and 5 miles (8km) wide. Surprisingly it has a network of 350 miles (560km) of lanes, giving it the feel of a much larger island. The most southerly of the British Isles, Jersey has more daily hours of sun than anywhere else in Britain. In summer the island has a daily average of eight hours of sunshine and an average maximum temperature of about 68°F (20°C). The best months to visit are from May to September, July and August being the hottest. Sea temperatures are chilly or refreshing, depending on your hardiness, averaging 62.8°F (17.1°C) in summer.

The Bailiwick of Jersey embraces two offshore reefs Les Minquiers, commonly known as the Minkies, 9 miles (14km) south of St Helier, and Les Ecréhous, 5 miles (8km) off the northeast coast. French adventurers occasionally attempt to take possession of the reefs and in 1950 the dispute over ownership was taken to the International Court in The Hague. The islands were awarded to Jersey – though French fishermen can still fish around the reefs.

## LANGUAGE

Until the Victorian era the common spoken language on the island was Jèrriais, a derivation of ancient Norman French. Large numbers of English settlers arrived on Jersey in the 19th century (many of them officers retired on half pay) and by the end of the century English was the prevalent language of St Helier. In all the country parishes, however, Jèrriais continued to be the main language until the 1960s. It is rarely heard these days but you might catch a few words from elderly locals in the countryside, perhaps at a market or agricultural auction. Only a handful of the population speak the patois fluently, but a concerted effort to revive interest in the language has led to the introduction of classes in some schools.

Jèrriais never enjoyed the status of standard French, or what was referred to as *le bouôn français*. This was used in churches, law courts and administration and even today a few words are used for prayers before the States (or local government), court sittings and in official documents. Some street names in St Helier still have their original French names alongside the English ones given by 19th-century settlers from mainland Britain; eg, the somewhat prosaic Church Street was La Rue Trousse Cotillon – Pick Up Your Petticoat Street.

## ECONOMY

The economy saw major changes during the late 20th century as the financial services industry took over from agriculture and tourism. The financial sector is

*Jersey is great for cycling*

now completely dominant, and the skyline of St Helier has seen a rash of high-rise HQs of banks, trusts, insurance and accountancy firms, along with a huge number of apartment blocks for financial workers. The Channel Islands have long attracted wealthy immigrants, seeking to benefit from the island's desirable lifestyle and advantageous tax laws. Only a handful are granted residency on Jersey each year through the High Value Residency initiative. Among the criteria is sufficient wealth to create tax for the Jersey States in excess of £145,000.

The tourist industry took off after World War II when sightseers arrived to see the relics of the German Occupation. The island's unique position as a holiday island close to France yet English speaking, with well-run hotels and guesthouses, made it a holiday paradise from the 1950s. Tourism reached its peak in the late 1980s, then low-budget airlines and package holidays to more exotic climes led to a decline in tourism for the comparatively costly Channel Islands. The finance service industry which forged ahead in the 1990s stifled tourism. Hotels were demolished or turned into financiers' flats, and the number of visitors declined. The financial services industry now accounts for over 40 percent of the total economic activity on Jersey, employing over a fifth of the workforce. But tourism may be crucial in the future and in an effort to lure back the holidaymakers, particularly the younger ones, accommodation has been revamped, the sports and spa scene have been rejuvenated and gastronomy is thriving. The long downward trend in travel to Jersey was reversed in 2018 when the island saw the highest number of visiting holidaymakers since 2001. Although the COVID-19 pandemic in 2020 and 2021 halted the development of tourism for a time, the aim is still to see one million visitors by 2030. However the cost of travel and accommodation in Jersey are still high in comparison to the Med – and you'll be lucky to get weather like sunny Spain.

# HISTORY AND CULTURE

It was around 6,500 BC that Jersey became an island, cut off from the land mass of Europe by rising sea levels. Its vulnerable location led to a long and turbulent history. Striking reminders of its past are dotted all over the island, from the prehistoric burial grave at La Hougue Bie to coastal fortifications against the French, and the chilling Jersey War Tunnels from the German Occupation.

Little evidence was left by the earliest invaders but, from 1204, when King John lost Normandy to France and the Channel Islands chose to remain loyal to the English crown, successive defences were built against the invaders from France. The most recent fortifications date from the German Occupation in World War II when Hitler gave orders for the island to be transformed into 'an impregnable fortress'.

## PREHISTORY

The earliest inhabited site on the island – and one of Europe's most important prehistoric sites – is La Cotte de St Brelade, a cave south of Ouaisné Bay, first occupied a quarter of a million years ago in the Lower Palaeolithic age. This sheltered site was inhabited intermittently for the next 200,000 years, but only during the colder months when the sea level was low enough to walk across from what is now France. The piles of woolly mammoth and rhino bones that were

### Ancient relics

On rare occasions when the sands have been washed away by storms, you can see the remains of ancient tree stumps in St Ouen's Bay. These are the relics of an early Neolithic forest, probably dating from the time when Jersey was linked to the continent.

*Dolmen entrance at La Hougue Bie*

discovered at the foot of the 98-ft (32-m) cliff suggested that the cave-dwellers stampeded herds of animals over the cliff to their deaths. Archaeological investigations, which started here in 1881, and continued on and off until 1978, also brought to light 13 teeth belonging to a Neanderthal man or woman. The cave is closed to the public, but crucial relics are displayed in the Jersey Museum and the archaeological gallery at La Hougue Bie.

By 8,000 BC the climate was milder and Guernsey, Alderney and Sark had become islands. It was another two thousand years before Jersey broke away, and humans migrated here. Neolithic farmers established settlements from around 4,000 BC, clearing woodland and creating fields for crops and herds of sheep and cattle. The most conspicuous evidence of these settlers are the dolmens and menhirs scattered around the island. An outstanding example is the passage grave at La Hougue Bie (see page 42).

During the Bronze and Iron ages, the Channel Islands had trade links with Britain, Ireland and France. An outstanding example of an import from this era is the 5-ft (1.4-m) long gold torque discovered in St Helier in 1888, and on display at the Jersey Museum.

The comparatively peaceful early Christian era was shattered by the Vikings who colonised Normandy. In 911 Rollo the Viking was made duke of Normandy on condition that he supported the king and protected the region from the invasions of other Vikings. The Duchy of Normandy expanded to the Channel Islands in 933 and the Normans made their mark with their feudal laws, seafaring traditions and language. An-oft quoted archaic Jersey law is the right to invoke *La Clameur de Haro,* a cry for justice said to be created by Rollo. If a civilian feels his property is being threatened he may go down on bended knee in the presence of two witnesses, and cry: *'Haro! Haro! Haro! A l'aide, mon prince, on me fait tort'* (O Rollo! O Rollo! To my aid, my prince, I am being wronged'), followed by

## ST HELIER – JERSEY'S PATRON SAINT

Born to pagan parents in Tongeren in modern-day Belgium, the hermit Helerius is said to have brought Christianity to Jersey. He arrived on the island in the 6th century, and founded a hermitage in a cave on a tidal islet where Elizabeth Castle stands today. For 15 years he devoted his life to prayer and to the protection of the small settlement of fishermen. In AD 555 Norman pirates landed on the islet, saw Helerius praying and cut off his head with axes – hence the two crossed axes on the emblem of St Helier. A monastery was founded here and Helerius was made a saint. His feast day is marked annually on the Sunday closest to 16 July by a pilgrimage to what is now known as Hermitage Rock.

the Lord's Prayer in French. No further action or trespass can be taken until judgement is given in the appropriate court of law. The *Clameur* is rarely invoked today – the last time it was used successfully was in 1980. In 1994 a Jersey resident raised the *Clameur* against his brother in the Royal Square, but it was incorrectly invoked and therefore ignored. If the *Clameur* is used without justification the claimant is fined.

## THE BRITISH CONNECTION

Following the victory of Norman Duke William II (William the Conqueror) at the Battle of Hastings, the Channel Islands became part of the Anglo-Norman realm. This was the beginning of the link with the English Crown, reinforced in 1204 when King John lost Normandy to France. The Channel Islands were given the choice of

*Hermitage Rock, home of St Helier*

*Harvesting seaweed at Gorey Harbour*

remaining loyal to the English Crown or reverting to France. They opted for the former, and in return the king granted them 'the continuance of their ancient laws and privileges', laying the foundation for self-government. Jersey was no longer a peaceful backwater – France, just across the water, became the foe.

## THE FRENCH THREAT

Fear of invasion from France led to the construction of coastal fortifications. In the early 13th century the great medieval fortress of Mont Orgueil was built to command the east coast, looking across to continental Normandy. 'Mount Pride' remained the chief stronghold of the island for nearly four centuries, but this was a bastion built for bows and arrows, and by the mid-16th century it was no longer up to defending the island. Work started on a new fortification on the islet of St Helier, built to withstand modern warfare and provide anchorage for the large merchant ships. Sir Walter

### States of Jersey

The States of Jersey, the island's parliament, first convened in the 16th century. Today it comprises the Lieutenant Governor, who is the Monarch's representative in the island, the Bailiff, the Dean of Jersey, the Attorney General and the Solicitor General – along with 10 senators, 12 parish constables and 29 deputies.

Raleigh, who resided here as the island's governor, named it Fort Isabella Bellissima (Elizabeth the most Beautiful) in tribute to his beloved queen, Elizabeth I.

During the English Civil War, Jersey hoped to remain neutral, but local rivalries led to the island's own brief civil war. The island finally emerged on the side of the king. The young Prince of Wales took refuge here briefly in 1646, and following the execution of his father, King Charles I in 1649, came back and was proclaimed King Charles II by the Governor of Jersey, Sir George Carteret. As a reward, Charles II bequeathed to Carteret a large tract of land in the American colonies, henceforth known as New Jersey. Jersey's loyalty to the monarch led to an inevitable invasion force of Parliamentarians under Cromwell. In 1651, 80 vessels crossed to Jersey with more than 2,500 troops under Admiral Blake. Royalist resistance was crushed and Cromwell's new model army controlled the island.

## NAVIGATION AND KNITTING

Following the restoration of the monarchy Jersey enjoyed a phase of comparative peace and prosperity. Shipbuilders grew rich on cod-fishing in Newfoundland, splendid merchants' houses (known as 'Cod Houses') were constructed in St Aubin, while inland agriculture flourished. Cider was produced in large quantities and exported, sheep were abundant and the majority of the islanders (including men and children) were knitting stockings and fishermen's sweaters. (Legend has it that Mary Queen of Scots went to her execution wearing a pair of white Jersey stockings). Knitting in fact became so popular and lucrative that the harvest crops and seaweed collection began to suffer. A new law was introduced in 1708 forbidding the making of stockings during harvest and *vraicing* (seaweed collecting). Islanders were made to work on the land 'on pain of imprisonment on bread and water and the confiscation of their work'.

## THE BATTLE OF JERSEY

Jersey's privateering activities in the 1770s, when ships were licensed to plunder enemy vessels, led to two attempts by France to capture the island – first in 1779, and more famously, in 1781.

*Locals gather for a court meeting, 1920*

*Detail from Outbreak of War at the Occupation Tapestry Gallery*

On 6 January, under the command of Baron de Rullecourt, 600 troops took the island completely by surprise, landing at La Rocque in the southeast corner of the island and marching as far as Royal Square. The lieutenant-governor, still in bed, was tricked into believing that the enemy had around 14,000 troops, and immediately surrendered. However, the heroic Major Francis Peirson, a local 24-year-old officer, ignored the surrender and led the local militia to victory in the Battle of Jersey. Both Peirson and De Rullecourt were killed in action. This was the last attempt by France to capture the island. For fear of further invasions 30 Martello towers were constructed around the island, and many of these survive.

## THE VICTORIAN ERA

French vessels continued to be victims of Jersey privateers, leading to Napoleon's outcry: 'France can tolerate no longer this nest of brigands and assassins. Europe must be purged of this vermin. Jersey is England's shame'. With Napoleon's defeat at Waterloo, wars with France finally ceased. Although knitting and cider-making saw a decline, fishing, shipbuilding and agriculture still flourished. The prosperity of the island attracted newcomers, many of them army and navy officers retired on half pay after the Napoleonic Wars. By 1840 up to 5,000 English had settled here and by the end of the 19th century English had become the prevalent language of St Helier.

## THE GERMAN OCCUPATION

The Channel Islands were the only British territory to fall into German hands during World War II. Tiny the islands may have been but Hitler saw them as the first step to his intended inva-sion of the United Kingdom. In 1940 Churchill decided that the islands, which had no strategic value for Britain, could not justify the cost of defence and the decision was taken that they should be demilitarised. Prior to the arrival of Hitler's troops 90,000 peo-ple fled the island while 80,000 decided to stay. Within two years Jersey was turned into an impregnable fortress, with thousands of foreign forced labourers and Russian prisoners-of-war toiling in harsh conditions to construct concrete walls, bunkers and gun emplacements. This was to be part of Hitler's Atlantic Wall project, a line of defence works extending all the way from the Baltic to the Spanish frontier. Over half a million tons of concrete were used around the coasts.

In the mistaken belief that an attack on the Channel Islands was imminent, Hitler gave orders for the construction of an emergency underground hospital for the treatment of German casualties – today's Jersey War Tunnels. Since the invasion never took place the hospital was never put to use. For the islanders the German Occupation was a time of hardship and deprivation, with shortages of food, fuel and medicines. During the last months the near-starving population was saved by the Swedish SS *Vega*, bringing Red Cross food parcels and other essential provisions. On 9 May 1945 British forces liberated the Channel Islands and the occupying forces surrendered peacefully. Citizens gathered to listen to Churchill's broadcast of the German capitulation: 'And our dear Channel Islands are to be freed today'. Liberation Day on 9 May has been celebrated ever since.

## POSTWAR DEVELOPMENTS

After the war, tourism was boosted by visitors from the UK, curious to see the after-effects of the Occupation. Tourism flourished up to the late 1980s, but has been stifled ever since by the finance industry. Stable government and advantageous tax laws led to the development of international financial services, including offshore banking, trust management and insurance. Today finance directly employs around 20 percent of the island's workforce and accounts for at least 40 percent of economic output.

Jersey is not part of the United Kingdom but a dependency of the British Crown, as it has been since 1204, with the islanders owing their allegiance to the Queen. The island is self-governing and has its own financial and legal systems and its own court of law. The island's parliament, known as the States of Jersey (see page 20), has been the subject of debate and argument for years. The introduction of ministerial government in 2005, adopted to replace the antiquated committee system, has had little positive effect and the States is as divided as ever. Political reforms are very much on the agenda but there is a long way to go before any consensus is reached on a new structure for the States. As the Channel Islands are not part of the EU, Brexit had no direct impact on their financial service industries and a limited impact on trade in goods.

# HISTORICAL LANDMARKS

**c.6,000 BC** Jersey becomes an island when it is separated from Europe.

**5,000–2,850 BC** Neolithic Period. Megalithic tombs or dolmens are erected, including La Hougue Bie.

**2,250–350 BC** Bronze and Iron ages.

**6th century AD** St Helier is martyred by pirates in 555.

**1066** Battle of Hastings. Channel Islands become part of the Anglo-Norman realm.

**1204** King John loses Normandy to France but the islands remain loyal to the English Crown and are granted self-government.

**1204** Work starts on Mont Orgueil Castle.

**1550–1600** Construction of Elizabeth Castle.

**1642–51** English Civil War. After a brief period of civil war, Jersey emerges on the side of the Royalists.

**1649** Charles I beheaded. Charles II (then Prince of Wales) takes refuge in Jersey and is proclaimed king by the governor.

**1651** Parliamentarians sent to put down Royalist resistance.

**1781** Battle of Jersey. The heroic Major Peirson leads the local militia to victory when the French attempt to take over the island.

**1940** Channel Islands demilitarised; 10,000 evacuated from Jersey.

**1940–44** German Occupation. Foreign prisoners brought to the island to build defences. Rationing introduced.

**1945** Liberation of the Channel Islands on May 9.

**1973** Britain joins the EEC (now the EU).

**2004** Jersey celebrates 800 years of allegiance to the Crown.

**2008** Haut de la Garenne, St Martin, becomes the focus of an ongoing investigation into historic child abuse

**2012** In the long-running issue of States reform, proposals are made to reduce the number of States Members.

**2018** Channel Islands sign deal with UK over post-Brexit trade

**2019** July temperatures break records in Jersey.

**2020** The COVID-19 pandemic leads to Jersey's lockdown.

**2021** Jersey gradually lifts COVID-19 restrictions.

Mont Orgueil Castle and Gorey Harbour

# OUT AND ABOUT

Jersey is a tiny island of 9 miles (14km) by 5 miles (8km), but the network of 350 miles (560km) of roads, many of them narrow lanes, plus the speed limit of 40 mph (64km/h) and even 15 mph (24km/h) on some rural roads gives the impression it's far bigger. The island is divided up into 12 parishes – not that you would be aware which one you were in when driving around the island. Each parish has its own stretch of coastline, and wherever you are based on the island you are never far from a good beach.

The land slopes from the dramatic cliffs on the north coast to the flat sandy beaches of the south. The capital and hub of the island is St Helier on the south coast, which is the best centre for shopping and bus transport to attractions and beaches. However, you may prefer smaller, prettier and less traffic-thronged resorts such as Gorey or St Aubin – or the beach resort of St Brelade. If you don't have your own car these three centres all have good bus connections.

The following pages start with St Helier and then take in some inland excursion destinations from the capital before going around the coast in a clockwise direction. Travelling from the south to north or north to south, often via picturesque valleys, is another option – but travelling east to west or vice versa is trickier unless you know the island well.

## ST HELIER

Capital of Jersey and its only real town, **St Helier ❶** took its name from the hermit, Helerius, who arrived here in the 6th century (see page 17). It was not until the 19th century that St Helier was developed as a main town with its harbours extended to become a commercial port. Today the first impressions are hardly picturesque.

Arriving by sea you are greeted by a power station, cranes, high-rise blocks and traffic-thronged streets. However, the centre of the capital reveals a more charming side with its markets, museums and pedestrianised streets. A good starting point is the **Jersey Tourism** Visitor Centre (www.jersey.com) which is located within Liberation Bus Station, just along the Esplanade from Liberation Square.

## LIBERATION SQUARE

It was in **Liberation Square A** that crowds of islanders gathered on 9 May 1945 to welcome the British fleet that had come to release them after five gruelling years of German Occupation. The **Liberation Sculpture**, representing islanders and a British soldier clutching the Union Jack, was placed here in 1995, the fiftieth anniversary of the Liberation when Prince Charles opened the square. The Union Jack which featured in the original sculpture was then changed to a group of doves by the Occupation and Liberation Committee. Following comments about islanders being more likely to eat the doves than release them (food shortages were severe during the Occupation) the Union Jack was reinstated. On the north side of the square the **Pomme d'Or Hotel** overlooking the harbour provided a prime site for the German Naval Headquarters during the Occupation. On Liberation Day, in front of crowds of islanders, the Union Jack was raised on the balcony of the building, replacing the Nazi swastika.

## JERSEY MUSEUM AND ART GALLERY

Just east of Liberation Square, the **Jersey Museum and Art Gallery B** (www.jerseyheritage.org; daily Jan–mid-Mar & Nov–Dec 10am–4pm, mid-Mar–Oct until 5pm) offers an excellent introduction to the island, tracing its story from prehistoric to present times. On the ground floor you can see some fascinating archive footage of the early years of tourism on the island, and a reconstruction of a

Paleolithic cave scene at La Cotte de St Brelade, where cave dwellers hunted animals by stampeding them off the clifftops. The first floor is devoted to the story of Jersey, and its culture and traditions, including oyster-catching, shipbuilding, farming, knitting and tourism. The most valued treasure is a Bronze Age flange-twisted torque, discovered in St Helier and thought to have been a gift from a tribal leader on the mainland to ensure the loyalty of an island chieftain. Adjoining the museum on the upper floors are the faithfully restored rooms of the Merchant's House, built in the 19th century for a wealthy merchant.

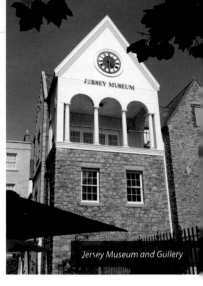
*Jersey Museum and Gallery*

## PARISH CHURCH OF ST HELIER

Just north of Jersey Museum the **Parish Church of St Helier** ⓒ was a nerve centre of the town in times gone by. A church has stood here since the 11th century and it was a place where locals sought refuge in times of crisis, elections were held and bells were rung when enemy ships were sighted. Below the pulpit a memorial is dedicated to the heroic Major Peirson, who was killed in nearby Royal Square in the Battle of Jersey; his enemy, the Baron de Rullecourt, has a stone memorial in the graveyard. On the far side of the churchyard, Church Street still retains its fetching French-Norman name alongside the English. La Rue Trousse Cotillon or 'Pick Up Your Petticoat Street' dates from the times when ladies had to lift up their dresses to avoid mud, drains and sewers. The street leads into Library Place, where the aptly named Constable of St Helier, Pierre le Sueur, who founded the underground sewage system, is honoured with an obelisk.

## ROYAL SQUARE

East of Church Street the peaceful, leafy **Royal Square** ⓓ was formerly the hub of town life. This used to be the marketplace, and it was here that proclamations were announced, prisoners awaited trial in a wooden cage and petty offenders were flogged or put in the pillory or stocks. In 1648 two witches were strangled and burnt at the stake in the square. Happier events take place these days, such as weddings (for UK as well as Jersey residents) in the former corn market. In the centre of the square a stone commemorates the Battle of Jersey (see

### THE JERSEY LILY

Two portraits of Jersey's most famous daughter, Lillie Langtry (1853–1929), herald the second-floor art gallery at the Jersey Museum. Born Emilie Charlotte LeBreton, daughter of a dean of Jersey, she married a wealthy widower, Edward Langtry, at the age of 21. They moved to London where she led the field in fashion and, on becoming the semi-official mistress of the Prince of Wales (later King Edward VII), the talk of the town. The portraits by Sir John Everett Millais, also a Jersey native, and Sir Edward Poynter, were both crowd-pullers at the Royal Academy in 1878 – a year after she had become the Prince of Wales' mistress. Lillie went on to become a highly successful actress – the first society woman to go on the stage. She took up American citizenship in 1897, divorced her husband, remarried and bought a ranch in California. She died in Monte Carlo and is buried in the graveyard in the church of St Saviour with the rest of her family.

page 21) which took place here in 1871. The conspicuous gilded statue is King George II (1727–60), dressed as Caesar – but wearing the Order of the Garter. He was given this place of honour after donating £300 for the construction of St Helier's first harbour and the square's name was changed from the Market Place to Royal Square.

The king's coat of arms can be seen above the entrance of the **Royal Court**, the island's court of justice, on the south side of the square. On 8 May 1945 the bailiff of Jersey stood on the balcony here in front of a seething mass of islanders and relayed Churchill's message that the Channel Islands were to be freed. The **States Chamber**, Jersey's Parliament, stands to the left of the Royal Court. If you look carefully at the paving stones in the west half of the square you will see a large 'V' for Victory, which was secretly inscribed by a local stonemason while relaying the flagstones during the latter stages of the Occupation. Discovery of such acts of subversion would often lead to deportation, and he hid the 'V' under a layer of sand. The letters 'EGA' and '1945' were later added to commemorate the arrival of the Swedish Red Cross Ship, SS *Vega*. Both occupiers and islanders by this stage were near starvation but it was only civilians who were allowed the parcels from the ship. The Germans just watched as excited local people ripped opened their packets of cheese, chocolate and dried eggs.

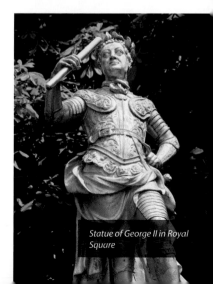

*Statue of George II in Royal Square*

*Jewellers and 17th-century houses in Royal Square*

## SHOPPING STREETS AND MARKETS

From Peirson Place beside the pub you can access **King Street**, which, with **Queen Street**, makes up the main pedestrianised shopping thoroughfare. As well as the usual High Street chain stores there are individual retail outlets, including a remarkable number of jewellers. At Charing Cross at the western end a large metal *crapaud* (the symbolic Jersey toad) sits atop a granite pillar. The sculpture marks the site of an 18th-century prison and is engraved with the crimes and punishments of the time. At the other end of the street turn right for Halkett Place and the **Central Market ⓔ** (Mon–Sat 7.30am–5.30pm) on the other side of the street. A wonderful array of fresh produce – strawberries, asparagus, Jersey herbs and home-grown flowers – is laid out in this splendid Victorian glass-roofed building. The central feature is an ornate three-tiered fountain where cherubic figures lean on water jars with their paddles and goldfish swim in the pool below. Apart from fruit and vegetable stalls there are butchers and bakeries, a delicatessen and a dairy shop with products from the famous Jersey cow and other Jersey specialities such as *nier beurre* or black butter (see page 103).

For the **Fish Market** (also known as Beresford Market, same hours as Central Market) exit Central Market on the far side and turn left for Beresford Street. The building is modern without the elegance of Central Market, but there's a great spread of fresh fish, both local and imported. From Jersey waters you can expect to find live lobster, spider- and chancre crabs, scallops, locally farmed oysters and mussels, and amongst the fish, mackerel, wrasse and grey mullet. If all this looks tempting and it's time for a break, try out one of the two eateries here for a fishy snack and glass of wine.

## JERSEY ARTS CENTRE AND THE GEORGIAN HOUSE

At the end of Beresford Street you'll come face to face with a group of life-sized bronze Jersey cattle, including a calf looking suspiciously at a tiny *crapaud* or toad (the island mascot). Just to the north the **Jersey Arts Centre** Ⓕ (www.artscentre.je) is a lively venue that hosts regular exhibitions of contemporary art, as well as concerts and theatre productions.

*Inside the Central Market*

West of Central Market The Georgian House at 16 New Street (Thu–Fri 10am–4pm) has been restored to its former elegance. Originally the home of a public notary, it has served as the head-quarters of the Liberty Gentlemen's Club and the workshop of De Gruchy, the Jersey department store. By the 1980s it was neglected and demolition was threatened. However the National Trust bought the property for £1 in 2003 and thanks to a £1 million bequest it was able to undertake a meticulous renovation.

## ALONG THE WATERFRONT

On New North Quay, across the busy A1 from Liberation Square, the **Maritime Museum** Ⓖ (www.jerseyheritage.org; Jan–mid-Mar & Nov–Dec Sun 10am–4pm, mid-Mar–Oct daily until 5pm) occupies a 19th-century warehouse. This first-rate museum brings to life Jersey's former role as a seafaring state. It was one of the largest shipbuilding centres in Europe, its shipyards around the coast producing over 800 wooden sailing ships in the mid-19th century. It is very much an interactive museum where you can feel the force of the sea, sail a ship, tie a sheepshank and listen to songs and salty tales of the past. Among the highlights are a

### KINGDOM OF CONGERS

The firm oily meat of the conger eel was regarded as a delicacy, and it used to be salted, dried and preserved throughout the winter. The conger-rich waters and the popularity of the eel led to the island's nickname in the 17th century: the Kingdom of Congers. The eel was sold to the wealthy, while the poor fisher-men were left with the bony head. This, however, was the key ingredient for a flavoursome fish soup, traditionally garnished with marigold petals.

full-size replica of the bow of the Jersey-built brig, the *Orient Star*, and the Voyage Globe, a giant animatronic globe illustrating the journeys of Jersey's ships all over the world. On Mondays, Tuesdays and Wednesdays you can watch volunteer boat builders repair and maintain the museum's fleet of historic vessels. Examples of the restored boats can sometimes be seen in the marina outside the museum.

*The Steam Clock*

The museum shares the building with the **Occupation Tapestry Gallery** (same opening hours and same entrance ticket as the Maritime Museum). The 12 richly-coloured tapestries depict scenes of the German Occupation, from the announcement of war, through deprivation and deportation to the arrival of Red Cross parcels and Liberation. These finely worked panels were designed and stitched by the islanders to commemorate the 50th anniversary of Liberation, with each of the 12 parishes submitting a tapestry.

Next to the museum on the east side you are unlikely to miss the world's largest **Steam Clock**, modelled on a 19th-century paddle steamer. The benches here and around the old harbour basin record local vessels and their builders. Some of the ships sailed the oceans of the world, others worked the North Atlantic and the triangular trading routes based on the cod-fisheries, while the smaller vessels plied their trade in home waters.

## THE WATERFRONT CENTRE

The whole waterside area to the west is known as **The Waterfront Centre**. After years of political wrangling, this development is still not complete, and what has gone up so far has been hugely controversial. This vast space by the sea, with so much potential, intended as 'the new maritime quarter reconnecting the town with the seashore' and to 'breathe new life into the town and the island, enriching the quality of life of resident and visitor alike' has been ruined by utilitarian high-rise buildings, car parks, and a huge carbuncle of a hotel right on the water's edge. The general feeling is that a huge potential has been sacrificed on the altar of the financial services sector, and that what could have been an attractive waterside, on the lines of other successful waterfronts in Europe, is doing little more than providing housing and parking for financiers. At the northern end **Les Jardins de la Mer Ⓗ**, gardens with a fountain, bring some light relief, and the terrace of La **Frégate Café** provides fine views of Elizabeth Castle.

## ELIZABETH CASTLE

Guarding the entrance of St Helier harbour, lies the great Tudor stronghold of **Elizabeth Castle ❶** (www.jerseyheritage.org); early Apr–Oct 10am–5.30pm, last admission 5pm), which defended the island for over 300 years. On an islet in St Aubin's Bay, the castle is connected to the shore by a causeway which you can cross at low tide. When the water is up the only means of access is the amphibious blue Castle Ferry (separate charge) which leaves at all tides from West Park slip (near Les Jardins de la Mer) and makes an enjoyable trip on a fine day.

By the late 16th century the great Mont Orgueil on Jersey's east coast was becoming increasingly vulnerable and a new fortification was required to meet the demands of modern-day warfare. Queen Elizabeth I ordered its construction and Sir Walter Raleigh, who lived here as governor, named it Fort Isabella Bellissima (Elizabeth the Most Beautiful) after his queen. The fortification was expanded several times in the 17th century, though this didn't prevent it coming under fire from mortars during the English Civil War. Philip Carteret, the then-governor, sustained a siege here for 50 days and in 1651 a mortar shell attack by the Parliamentarians forced the Royalists to surrender. Charles II took refuge here on two occasions, once as Prince of Wales, and again, three years later, after the execution of his father, when he was proclaimed King Charles II. During World War II the Germans added to the fortification with bunkers, gun batteries and a command post at the top of the castle.

Visitors can explore the battlements and bunkers, climb up to the oldest fortress of the Upper Ward and discover **Hermitage Rock**, home of St Helier, Jersey's patron saint (see page 17). Buildings around the Parade Ground house exhibitions covering the history of the garrison, the development of the cannon and the story of

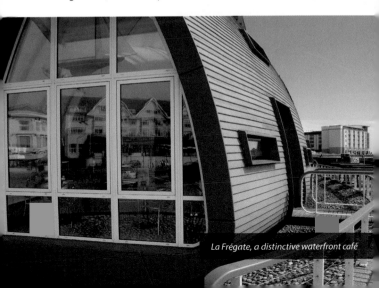

*La Frégate, a distinctive waterfront café*

*Elizabeth Castle at night*

the Jersey Royal Militia. On regular days throughout the season history is kept alive by displays of artillery, military parades and the firing of the noonday cannon. There is plenty of audience participation and visitors may be dragooned into drill practice and marching the Parade Ground!

## FORT REGENT

The final fortress built on Jersey was **Fort Regent ❶**, whose location is marked by the white spaceship-like dome above the town and visible from Elizabeth Castle. Fears of further French invasion led to its construction in 1806–14 but it was never needed to defend the island. The building was converted into a huge leisure centre in 1958 with sports facilities, concert hall, exhibitions and entertainment. Today it offers a PlayZone for children, a sports club and occasional concerts and events.

# EXCURSIONS FROM ST HELIER

## JERSEY WAR TUNNELS

Following the Führer's orders to turn the Channel Islands into 'an impregnable fortress', slave workers were put to work on creating command posts and gun emplacements around the island. The most evocative of all these German fortifications is the **Jersey War Tunnels ❷** (Les Charrières Malorey, St Lawrence; www.

jerseywartunnels.com; Mar–Nov, daily 10am–4pm), the vast underground complex of Ho8 (Höhlgangsanlage 8). By car, take the A1 west out of St Helier, turn right on to the A11 at Bel Royal, then follow the signs for the War Tunnels. Alternatively you can take Liberty Bus Route 8 from Monday to Saturday all year, Route 28 from April to September or one of the vintage shuttle buses (with commentary), all from Liberty Bus Station, St Helier (www.libertybus.je).

Hundreds of forced labourers from all over Europe, including Russian and Polish prisoners-of-war, were used to create a complex of bomb-proof barracks to protect the garrison of around 12,000 men against assault from sea or air. The project involved 16 tunnels, requiring the excavation of thousands of tonnes of rock and 6,000 tonnes of concrete to line the tunnels. Work came to a halt in 1943 when news came through of an impending Allied invasion of Europe, and orders were given for the complex to be turned into a huge subterranean casualty clearing station. The wards, operating theatre and administrative rooms were to cater for hundreds of wounded. The allied landings never happened, the German forces surrendered peacefully on 9 May 1945 and the unused Ho8 was taken over by a British medical unit and virtually stripped of all its contents. A year later it opened to sightseers and souvenir-seekers.

Hospital scenes within the long, dark and chilly tunnels

*Operating theatre at the Jersey War Tunnels*

Garden of Reflection at the War Tunnels

have been reconstructed and a combination of archive film footage, islanders' reminiscences, photos and poignant correspondence chart life under the Nazis. The exhibits bring home the hardship endured by slave labourers (at least 560 died in the Channel Islands), the deprivation of islanders and the fate of those who were deported to camps in Germany. The site also incorporates the **Garden of Reflection**, designed for visitors to contemplate the suffering during the Occupation; and the **War Trail**, covering land once used as an artillery battery, and now being reclaimed by nature.

## HAMPTONNE COUNTRY LIFE MUSEUM

In the heart of rural Jersey is the **Hamptonne Country Life Museum** ❸ (La Rue de la Patente, St Lawrence; www.jerseyheritage.org; daily mid-Mar–Oct 10am–5pm), which takes you back to farming life as it was three centuries ago. The most scenic route there is via **Waterworks Valley**: follow the A1 from St Helier until you are about half way round St Aubin's Bay, then turn inland at the C118. A refreshing antidote to frenetic St Helier, this is a peaceful green valley whose streams used to power six watermills. Today the island's main reservoirs are located here; beyond the Dannemarche Reservoir, fork left on to the C119 for the museum. It can also be reached by bus No 7.

A cluster of farm buildings has been faithfully restored and there are meadows, woodland and orchards to explore. Two houses have been recreated to demonstrate the living conditions of farming families in the 17th and 18th centuries. Expect a spinner, lacemaker, blacksmith or a 'goodwyf' in period costume who will tell tales of the English Civil War or entertain you with local gossip from the old farming community. The refurbished Syvret House gives an insight into 1940s rural life including farming traditions, day-to-day family life, language, religion and the German Occupation. The nearby cider barn houses

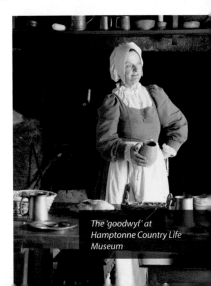

the apple crusher and twin-screw apple press that are still used every autumn to make cider. Children can meet the Hamptonne pigs, feed the chickens, follow a nature trail or test their knowledge with activity sheets or puzzles. (see page 102) – or you can order a picnic to enjoy in the orchards or meadows (tel: 01534 863955 in advance).

## ORCHID FOUNDATION

Horticultural enthusiasts should not miss the **Eric Young Orchid Foundation** ❹ (Victoria Village, Trinity;

*The 'goodwyf' at Hamptonne Country Life Museum*

*One of the Hamptonne rooms used in filming Under the Greenwood Tree*

www.ericyoungorchid.org; Feb–Nov Wed–Sat 10am–4pm) which displays an award-winning collection of orchids within a purpose-built nursery and exhibition complex. The late Eric Young first established his collection in Jersey in 1958 and within a decade it was recognised as one of the leading private collections in Europe. The complex features permanently planted landscapes that use raised beds, traditional Jersey granite, logs and branches to show the orchids in all their splendour. The nursery is not a commercial outfit, but there are often a few orchids for sale.

## LA HOUGUE BIE

One of the largest and best-preserved Neolithic passage graves in Europe, **La Hougue Bie** ❺ (La Route de la Hougue Bie, Grouville; www.jerseyheritage.org; mid-Mar–Oct daily 10am–5pm, last admission 4pm) has been a centre of activity for 6,000 years. To get there by car, take the A6 or A7 from St Helier to the Five Oaks roundabout, then turn right on to the B28 and follow the signs for La Hougue Bie. It is also served by bus Nos 21 and 13. If on arrival you're wondering where the monument is, head for the huge grassy mound. This conceals a rubble cairn which was built on top of the dolmen and faced with dry-stone walling. Centuries later Christianity made its mark on the site by the construction of two little chapels on top of the mound.

Following the Reformation the site passed into private hands and Philippe d'Auvergne, the duke of Bouillon, converted the ruined chapels into a neo-Gothic folly that became known as The Prince's Tower. A hotel was added in the 19th century and the site became one of the island's first tourist attractions, complete with pleasure garden, bowling alleys and fine views. Excavations in 1924 necessitated the demolition of the hotel and tower and led to the discovery of a low passage leading to funeral chambers.

The roof height of the tunnel-like passage grave is only 5ft (1.4m), so you have to stoop to gain access to the funereal chamber. Built of huge blocks of stone topped by capstones, this dark, mysterious – and far from spacious – chamber would have been used for ritual and ceremonial functions, as well as for burials. Fragments of human and animal bones, along with flint arrowheads and pottery

*Award-winning orchids*

Dolmen entrance, La Hougue Bie

fragments, were discovered here during excavation. Limpet shells were found on top of the capstones; these could have had a religious significance – or they might have just been the leftovers from the dolmen builders' lunch.

A pathway leads up to the two restored chapels at the top of the mound. The **Chapel of Notre Dame de la Clarté** (Our Lady of the Dawn) was built in the late 12th century in alignment with the dolmen, suggesting that its Christian creators recognised the link between the ancient monument and the equinoctial alignment. In the 1520s Dean Mabon (see box) added what became known as the **Jerusalem Chapel**, where, if you switch on the lights, you can see the faint outlines of two archangels.

During the Occupation in World War II a battalion command bunker was built on the Hougue Bie site, beside the burial mound. This now houses a memorial to the workers who were brought to the Channel Islands from Europe to work on the German fortifications. In one section the words of the slave labourers and their guards are recorded on metal plaques; in another the names of 503 victims are inscribed on a glass pillar.

Also on the site are galleries of geological and archaeological displays, highlights of which are animal remains from La Cotte de St Brelade (see page 15), jadeite axe-heads that were traded across to Europe in 3000 BC, and rare hordes of Iron and Bronze Age coins.

## SAMARÈS MANOR

Fourteen acres (6 hectares) of gorgeous landscaped gardens are the highlight of **Samarès Manor** ❻ (www.samaresmanor.com; early Apr–Oct daily 9.30am–4.30pm) in St Clement's, southeast of St Helier (access either by car or bus No 1a). The name Samarès derives from the old Norman French *Salse Marais*, or saltwater marsh, dating from ancient times when the owners profited from the saltpans on the low-lying land to the south. The grounds were originally designed in the 1920s by Sir James Knott, a shipping magnate and philanthropist, who spent the last 10 years of his life here. Knott's passion was plants from the East, hence the Japanese Garden, Exotic Border, rock and water gardens and large ponds with islands and camellia plantations.

Bordering the manor house is a delightful walled garden

### Holy sepulchre

In the 1520s Dean Mabon, who had made a pilgrimage to the Holy Land, had a shrine built under the Jerusalem Chapel in imitation of the Holy Sepulchre in Jerusalem. According to a Protestant chronicler of the late 16th century, the dean claimed to receive visions of the Virgin Mary and staged fake miracles to encourage alms from pilgrims.

*Samarès Manor surrounded by extensive gardens*

full of culinary, cosmetic and medicinal herbs. The former bring flavour to dishes served in the Herb Garden Café (also good for cream teas). Plants in the gardens with a red marker can be purchased and taken back to the UK. The nursery has been expanded and offers a good choice of plants for sale. Samarès specialities are roses, herbs, hardy perennials and lavender – as well as favourites such as the Jersey agapanthus, ice plants and Echium (bee plants). Visitors can take a guided tour of the herb garden at the **Jersey Rural Life Museum** and, from Monday to Saturday (extra charge), of the privately owned **manor house**. Children will probably prefer the play area and the farm animals dotted about the surrounding fields and paddocks.

## THE SOUTHWEST

From St Helier a vast crescent of south-facing sands extends all the way to the picturesque port and resort of St Aubin's in the west. A headland with glorious bay views divides the port from St Brelade, where palm-fringed gardens overlook one of the finest beaches on the island. From here you can walk along the clifftops to the dramatically located Corbière Lighthouse. Cyclists, joggers or walkers can cover the southwestern corner of the island by following the route of the old Jersey Railway line. Opened in 1870, this ran from St Helier to St Aubin, following the bay, and was then extended to Corbière. The track was turned into a footpath after competition from buses led to the closure of the railway and in 1936 fire destroyed much of the rolling stock at St Aubin.

## ST AUBIN'S BAY

Stretching from Elizabeth Castle to St Aubin, the bay is a long sweep of sheltered, unbroken sands. During spring tides the

*Portelet Bay viewed from Noirmont Point*

water laps the seawall, then retreats over 300m to expose a huge expanse of flat sands – so flat and expansive it was used for take-off and landings of De Havilland Dragons before Jersey's airport opened in 1937. St Aubin's is not the prettiest of the island's beaches, and it's a long trek through shallow waters to swim, but the sea is normally calm and safe for children and water sports are plentiful.

The beach between West Park and First Tower was once the site of the island's largest shipbuilders. In the 1860s Jersey was one the largest ship-building centres in the British Isles. Further west, halfway round the bay on the A1 inland, St Matthew's Church at Millbrook is known as the **Glass Church** (Mon–Fri 9am–5pm, Sun 1.30-5pm; free). The austere-looking church was built in 1840 but only attracted attention after the Parisian glass designer,

St Aubin and its harbour

René Lalique, embellished its interior in 1930s. He was commissioned by Lady Trent as a memorial to her husband, Jessie Boot, of Boots the Chemist. Panels, pillars, windows, the altar cross and the Art Deco angels are all rendered in opalescent glass, giving a soft glow to the church interior.

> **Salted fish**
>
> At St Aubin, during spring tides, razor fish can be enticed from the sands by sprinkling salt on the key-hole shaped opening at the top of their burrow. They think it's the tide coming in.

## ST AUBIN

You wouldn't think it now but **St Aubin** ❼ was the island's commercial hub from the early 16th to the 18th centuries. Fishermen used to set off from here in small boats to cross the Atlantic in spring, returning in autumn with rich stocks of Newfoundland cod. The fish was dried and salted, then shipped to the Mediterranean and Central America, to be traded for wines, spirits and tobacco. Merchants who made fortunes from fishing and shipbuilding built grand four-storey houses (known as 'cod houses') along the shore or in steep narrow streets, some of which you can still see today.

Named after the 5th-century Bishop of Angers, protector against piracy, St Aubin ironically also acquired much of its wealth through profiteering during the English Civil War. Jersey was pro-Royalist and the local ships were licensed to capture boats belonging to the enemy. Booty from these attacks was stashed away in the Old Court House Inn overlooking the harbour, now a historic hotel and restaurant. The building may look familiar to *Bergerac* fans – it featured as The Royal Barge in the cops-and-robbers series back in the 1980s.

St Aubin today is a picturesque port, popular for its villagey atmosphere, seaside strolls and ample choice of quayside eateries.

At low tide you can walk out to **St Aubin's Fort** (closed to the public), originally built in the 1640s to ward off French invaders and extended over the centuries. The last to leave their mark on the fort were the Germans during the World War II Occupation.

## NOIRMONT AND PORTELET

A steep hill from St Aubin (A13) takes you through a wooded valley west towards St Brelade's Bay. Just after the hairpin bend you are unlikely to miss the **Shell Garden** decorated with thousands of seashells but no longer open to the public. The next left turn brings you south to **Noirmont Point ❽**, a windswept headland, once known as Niger Mons or Black Hill, after the dark clouds that gather here. Sitting on the clifftop is a huge German command bunker (occasional openings May–Oct, check www.cios.org.je),

*View of St Brelade's Bay from Portelet Common*

extending to a depth of 40ft (12m) on two floors with a large observation tower. Views from here encompass St Aubin's Bay and on a really clear day you can spot the coast of Brittany on the horizon.

To the west lies **Portelet Bay ❾**, an inviting beach with soft sands and a sheltered setting, accessed down a long flight of steps from the clifftop car park at the Old Portelet Inn. The offshore Ile au Guerdain, topped by a defensive tower, became known as Janvrin's Tomb after an unhappy episode in its history. Janvrin was a sea captain who was refused landing at St Aubin's harbour when returning from plague-infested Nantes in Brittany in 1721. Janvrin then fell victim to the plague, and had to be buried on the island. His body was later transferred to St Brelade's cemetery. The tower on the islet was built over the grave in 1808 as one of the many fortifications against possible invasions during the Napoleonic Wars.

## OUAISNÉ AND ST BRELADE'S BAYS

**Portelet Common**, west of Portelet Bay, is a 77-acre (31-hectare) nature reserve set on the clifftop, affording dramatic sea views across to St Brelade's Bay. Below the slopes on the north-facing side of the common lies La Cotte de St Brelade (closed to the public), a major Palaeolithic site (see page 15). To the west, sea views stretch to the far end of St Brelade's Bay. Below is **Ouaisné** (prounounced 'Waynay') **Bay**, a spacious, sandy beach (accessed by a steep path from the common or by road) which is rarely crowded, even in midsummer. Behind the beach, the gorse-covered common is home to some rare species of fauna, including the Jersey green lizard, the agile frog and the Dartford warbler – though you would be lucky to spot them.

**St Brelade's Bay ❿** lies beyond the rocky promontory and is accessed across the beach at low tide, or over the rocks when the water is up. This is justifiably Jersey's most popular beach resort: a large crescent of gently sloping, southern-facing sands,

The Perquage from St Brelade's to the harbour

with clear blue waters and water sports galore. You can choose from blokarting (also called sand karting), stand-up paddle boarding, kayaking, coasteering, bodyboarding, windsurfing, water-skiing, dinghy sailing, skim boarding and surfing. The newest addition is paddle surf, once practised by the beach boys of Waikiki. The sport involves standing on a surfboard and using a long-handled oar to propel yourself forward to catch the waves. Above the bay, a boardwalk is flanked by cafés, restaurants and bucket-and-spade shops. Neat and colourful palm-lined gardens border the promenade while the slopes behind are dotted with the immaculate mansions of multimillionaires.

## CHURCHES OF ST BRELADE

Away from the crowds at the far west of the bay, the parish **Church of St Brelade** ⓫ overlooks the tiny harbour. The large churchyard was formerly the burial place of more than 300 Germans, some of whom had been prisoners here in World War I, others who had served during the more recent German Occupation. The bodies were exhumed in the early 1960s and given a final resting place at a military cemetery in St Malo across the water. The pink granite church dates back to the 11th and 12th centuries and still retains Norman features. As you go in, switch on the lights at the left of the entrance to reveal the enchanting interior with its warm granite walls. Embedded within them are beach stones and limpet shells.

Just next door to the church is the lovely **Fishermen's Chapel** ⑫, also built of local granite and dating back to Norman times. Following the Reformation it fell into disuse for some 300 years, and was variously used as an armoury, store room and carpenter's shop. Restoration in the early 20th century revealed a series of medieval frescoes depicting scenes from the Old and New Testaments. Only fragments remain but information boards fill in the gaps so you can make out the scenes. The most complete and the oldest fresco is the *Annunciation* on the east wall, which includes the members of the donor's family kneeling on either side of the Virgin and Archangel.

## JERSEY LAVENDER FARM

Follow your nose inland from St Brelade's Bay for **Jersey Lavender** ⑬ (Rue du Pon Marquet, St Brelade's; www.jerseylavender.co.uk; end Apr–mid-Oct Tue–Sun 10am–5pm, closed Mon), whose 9

### PATH TO FREEDOM

The granite stairway from St Brelade's churchyard to the tiny harbour is one of the last remaining sections of a Perquage, or sanctuary path. In the pre-Reformation era criminals who sought refuge in a parish church and swore to leave the island and give away all their possessions could use one of the Perquage walks, which linked each parish church to the sea. From there they would take a boat and seek sanctuary in France. The Perquages ceased to exist in 1683 when King Charles II bequeathed them to Sir Edward de Carteret, Viscount of Jersey, who then sold the land to farmers who owned the neighbouring fields.

*Fishermen's Chapel*

acres (3.6 hectares) of sweet-scented lavender resemble a little patch of Provence. The garden contains around 80 different varieties of lavenders, plus more than 100 kinds of culinary, medicinal, aromatic and dyers' herbs. The lavender is cut by hand, distilled on site and the essential oils matured and blended with other ingredients to produce eaux de toilette and colognes, soap and lotions and lavender bags. A video presentation shows all the stages of production and in summer there are tours of the farm. The best time to visit is between early June and late July/early August when the lavender is in flower – at other times of year the admission charge is substantially reduced. Lavender products are on sale in the shop – for a list of all the therapeutic usages of lavender oil, go to the website – and for all-day refreshments and home-made cakes, try Sprigs Café next to the shop.

## BEAUPORT

The steep road westwards from St Brelade's Bay takes you to **Beauport** ⑭, the islanders' favourite beach. Hidden away from the main road, entailing a longish trek down a steep hill, this beautiful sheltered bay is totally unspoilt. The waters here are crystal-clear, the soft sands washed by the tides and unspoilt by beach facilities. There is not even a drinks kiosk, let alone parasols – so remember to take your own provisions, along with sun cream.

# THE WEST COAST

This is Jersey's wildest coast, with waves crashing around Corbière Lighthouse and Atlantic surf pounding the huge beach of St Ouen's. This 4-mile (6.5km) arc of sand stretches almost the entire length of the west coast. Behind the beach a large expanse of unspoilt sand dunes is home to a wealth of flora and fauna.

## LA CORBIÈRE

Sitting atop the jagged rocks, **Corbière Lighthouse** ⑮ is one of Jersey's most familiar landmarks and a favourite spot from which to watch sunsets and rough seas. The name Corbière derives from *corbeau* (crow), traditionally seen as a bird of ill omen, and this wild and desolate tip of the island is inextricably linked with tales

Beauport Beach

of shipwrecks and smuggling. The first recorded ship to flounder on the rocks here was a Spanish vessel in 1495 carrying a cargo of wine. The seigneur of St Ouen was entitled by Jersey law to shipwrecked vessels and their cargo, and it is said that smugglers worked alongside the seigneur, luring ships on to the treacherous rocks with lanterns, which looked like the lights of vessels on the open sea. Among other casualties at Corbière was the Royal Mail Steam Packet, which was shipwrecked on the rocks in 1859. A lighthouse was finally erected here in 1874 – the first one in the British Isles to be made of reinforced concrete rather than stone. Weather permitting, the light beam can be seen from a distance of up to 18 miles (29km). The lighthouse is closed to the public.

At mid to low tide you can cross the causeway to the lighthouse, but check the tides before doing so and heed the siren which sounds when the waters start galloping up over the rocks. The monument of two clasped hands on the headland commemorates the rescue in 1995 of the French catamaran, *Saint Malo*, which ran aground when travelling from Jersey to Sark. All 307 passengers were saved. A carved stone on the causeway recalls a story with a less happy outcome: an assistant lighthouse keeper who drowned while trying to save a tourist caught by the incoming tide.

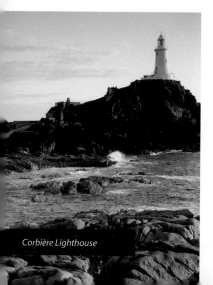

*Corbière Lighthouse*

## ST OUEN'S BAY

This huge sandy beach is Jersey's surfing hotspot. While La Pulente at the southern end is protected from the Atlantic swell, the big rollers further north provide championship conditions. Surf schools dotted along the bay hire out equipment for wind-surfing, bodyboarding and skim-boarding as well as surfing. Inexperienced surfers should always keep between the red and yellow flags, where Australian lifeguards patrol. A couple of cafés provide sea-view terraces where you can sit and watch the pros at play over hearty breakfasts, lunches or sunset suppers.

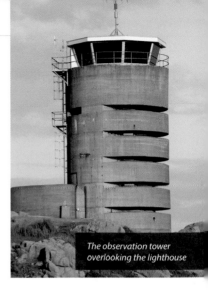

*The observation tower overlooking the lighthouse*

On a rocky islet at the southern end of the bay, **La Rocco Tower** ⑯ was one of nine round towers that were constructed along the bay during the Napoleonic Wars. The tower took a battering during the Occupation in World War II when the Germans used it as target practice, but it has since undergone restoration. The concrete wall backing the entire bay was built by slave labourers of the Todt Organisation against tanks coming ashore from Allied landing craft. Today the west-facing wall is a useful barrier during spring tides, and provides a warm, wind-free screen for sunbathers. The spacious sands here are favourite spots among islanders for post-surf barbecues, ideally as the sun is setting. Another of the round towers still standing is the squat **Kempt Tower** ⑰ (1834) further north, one of the few surviving examples of a Martello tower.

### Rooms with a view

Set on the cliff top overlooking Corbière Lighthouse, the massive concrete observation tower was built during the German Occupation in World War II. Restored in Modernist Bauhaus style, the six-floor tower, with terrific 360 degree views from the panoramic windows of the lounge/diner, is now rented out by Jersey Heritage as stylish self-catering accommodation.

At the southern end of the bay **Les Blanches Banques** sand dunes, where the marram grass is abundant, are a true haven for naturalists. Making their homes here are rare and aptly-named invertebrates such as the large Jersey green lizard, the blue winged grasshopper, and bloody-nosed beetle, whose name comes from the fact that when threatened, it secretes foul red liquid from its mouth which looks alarmingly similar to a drop of blood. More than 400 plant species have been recorded, no fewer than 16 of them featuring in the British red data book of endangered species.

In 1914 Jersey was called on to build a prisoner-of-war camp to accommodate 1,000 German prisoners. This was built on the lower dune plain, and by 1917 had expanded to take in 1,500 prisoners. The camp was closed in 1919.

Further north **Le Noir Pré** meadows, accessed from the Chemin de L'Ouzière, are one of the last strongholds of the loose-flowered or Jersey orchid (*Orchis laxiflora*). Guernsey is the only other place in the British Isles where the orchid can be found. In May to mid-June the meadows are a riot of colour from these and other flowering orchids. The reed beds and marshy surrounds of the nearby St Ouen's Pond (La Mare au Seigneur) draw scores of migratory birds, including sedge warblers and bearded reedlings. Marsh harriers can often be seen drifting over the reed beds.

# CHANNEL ISLANDS MILITARY MUSEUM

The Grande Route des Mielles (otherwise known as Five Mile Road, even though in reality it is only a little over three miles long) runs along Jersey's west coast from Les Laveurs to the St Peter/St Brelade boundary. It leads north to a clutch of visitor attractions. Above the beach a World War II German bunker is home to the **Channel Islands Military Museum** ⓲ (mid-Apr–Oct daily 10am–5pm), devoted to German Occupation memorabilia. Exhibits include arms and ammunition, Luftwaffe brass band instruments, tins of dried eggs from Red Cross food parcels and a stark notice of the sentence of death of a Jersey resident for releasing a pigeon with a message for England.

## STOCKING UP ON SEAWEED

If you happen to be on the beach in autumn or winter you may see tractors loading up with vraic (pronounced 'rack') from the beach. This is the seaweed which for centuries has been used to fertilise farms bordering the coast. There are two types of vraic: the weed washed up on the beach after stormy weather, and the type cut from the rocks, which was used as fuel by fishermen who could not afford coal or wool. Vraic collection days were party-like, with whole families gathering on the beaches, men wading out to the rocks on foot or going by boat, while women and children collected ormers, crabs and limpets in profusion. Spirits were kept high with vraic buns and cider, and at the end of the day the seaweed was brought up from the bay by horse and cart, and families returned home to feast on shellfish. Cutting of vraic from the rocks was only allowed at certain times of year, and was closely supervised by parish officials. Today there are no restrictions on the public removing seaweed and it is permitted to take a vehicle on to the beach for this purpose.

*Kempt Tower*

Across the main road buses disgorge visitors at **Jersey Pearl**, where you can learn all about pearls, watch the craftsmen and tour the plush showroom.

## L'ETACQ

The B35 then heads inland, and the road drops down to Le Grand Etacquerel, a vast expanse of reefs, better suited to rock pool exploration than swimming. A forest close to L'Etacq was submerged when the sea level rose after the Ice Age, and on rare occasions, when the sands have been washed away by storms, you can see the remains of ancient tree stumps. The main attraction is the **Faulkner Fisheries**, at the far end of the bay which sell ready-cooked lobster, crabs and fresh fish from an ex-German bunker. You can also enjoy fresh and affordable barbecued seafood at their wooden benches overlooking the coast. The bunker overlooks **Le Pulec Bay**, known familiarly as Stinky Bay for reasons that will soon become apparent. The odorous seaweed is still used to fertilise some of the Jersey Royal potatoes grown on the steeply sloping hillsides (*côtils*) on the landward side.

The windswept clifftops between L'Etacq and Grosnez provide some spectacular views along the coastline. The main road diverts inland after L'Etacq but you can pick up a footpath to the top of the cliffs. Wartime relics include restored gun emplacements and bunkers from the **Moltke Battery**, which once sprawled across the headland here. (Open some Sundays; for information visit www.cios.org.je). Perched right above the sea on rapidly eroding cliffs is **Le Pinacle** ⑲, a 200ft (60m) high menhir-like stack, used as an ancient ceremonial site from the Neolithic to Roman eras. Brooding on the clifftops to the north is the **MP3 direction and range-finding tower**, another potent symbol of the German Occupation. Inland the extensive windswept heath, known as **Les Landes**, is home to Jersey's racecourse, a rifle range and an airfield for model aircraft.

## GROSNEZ CASTLE

On the northwest tip of the island, the ruins of **Grosnez Castle** ⑳ stand evocatively on the heather- and gorse-clad clifftops. This was a 14th-century fortification believed to have been destroyed by the French in the same century. On a clear day you can spot all the other Channel Islands from the castle ruins. Going from left to right these are Guernsey, Jethou, Herm and Sark, with Alderney in the far distance and the coast of Normandy to the east. At low tide you can see an extensive reef, known as the Paternoster, offshore to the east. Local legend relates that in the 16th century a boatload of women and children, who were en route to colonise Sark, were shipwrecked on the treacherous rocks here. Superstitious sailors would recite the Lord's Prayer when rounding the reef, hence the name.

# THE NORTH COAST

The wild and rugged north coast, where cliffs tower above tiny sheltered harbours, couldn't be more of a contrast to the flat beaches and calm seas of the south. The peaceful north coast footpath (see page 90), stretching all the way from Grosnez in the west to Rozel in the east, is the most exhilarating walk on the island, affording spectacular sea views. The paths, flanked by wild flowers, dip down to little bays, where you can take a break at harbour-side cafés or cool off in clear waters.

## PLÉMONT

The most westerly beach is **Plémont Bay** ㉑ or, more correctly, La Grève au Lançon (Sand Eel Beach). At high tide the beach is non-existent, but twice a day the waters recede to reveal an unspoilt expanse of golden sands. This is by far the best beach on the north coast, and the longish flight of steps down and the lack of facilities keep away the crowds. The seas can get rough here, and it's popular with surfers, but normally in summer it's safe enough for bathing, and lifeguards patrol the beach for most of the day. Behind the beach the sea has eroded the cliffs; there are caves to explore and rock pools for paddling. The **Plémont Beach Café** at the top of the steps is an excellent spot for a bite, using prime Jersey produce. Parking just above the bay, where cars are lined up on the steep and narrow road, is best avoided in season. It's easier to leave your car near the bus stop at the top and take the scenic cliff path down to the beach, enjoying the views as you go.

For years the headland above the bay was the site of a derelict Pontins Holiday Camp, which was then purchased by a commercial company who wanted to build a large development. Jersey residents heaved a sigh of relieve when the National Trust successfully campaigned against the project and the land was sold to the Trust.

The old holiday camp was demolished and the beautiful headland restored to its natural state.

## GRÈVE DE LECQ

Going eastwards Grève de Lecq (well signed off the B55) is the most popular of the north coast bays, with a large car park to accommodate island tour buses, a sandy beach, fishing pier and choice of eateries. Up from the bay the **Grève de Lecq Barracks** ㉒ (closed to the public) were built in 1810–15 in preparation for an expected Napoleonic invasion. British troops were garrisoned here until the 1920s. The only surviving barracks on the island, they have been restored by Jersey's National Trust, and the old officers' quarters have been turned into self-catering accommodation for tourists.

*Catch of the day at Faulkner Fisheries*

*Colourful cottages at Rozel*

In a valley up the road the **Moulin de Lecq** is the place for a pint (see page 109), either in the garden or in the olde-worlde bar where the huge cog of this former water mill provides an unusual backdrop. The great water wheel outside still functions, though it is no longer used to grind flour. During the German Occupation the water wheel was used to power energy for searchlights to defend the bay.

The promontory east of the bay, known as **Le Câtel de Lecq**, was an Iron Age earthwork fortification, where Gallic and Roman coins were discovered. Beyond, a remote and extremely pretty beach, **Le Val Rouget**, can be accessed via a cliff path and a long dark tunnel, which you can only pass through at very low tide. The route goes via **Venus' Pool**, where you can jump from a high rock into the deep, dark waters. Youngsters love the adventure but check with locals about the tides and the route before setting off.

## LA MARE WINE ESTATE

From Grève de Lecq the B40 takes you to the village of St Mary; from here follow signs for the Devil's Hole to reach **La Mare Wine Estate** ㉓ (www.lamarewineestate.com; Apr–Oct Mon–Sat 9.30am–5.30pm; 6 tours a day from 10.45am–3.30pm). From a small family-run tourist attraction, it has expanded into a professionally managed 25-acre (10-hectare) estate, producing a range of wines, ciders and spirits – along with a large selection of Jersey culinary specialities. The estate is centred around an old granite farmhouse and tours cover the vineyards and orchards, distillery, chocolate kitchen and a tasting session. Forty thousand bottles are produced annually, including sparkling wines, made according to the *méthode Champenoise*, and a range of still whites and reds. Most of the cider made here is double distilled in a Cognac brandy pot and aged in oak casks to become Jersey apple brandy. The vineyard shop stocks black butter (see page 103), preserves and luxury chocolates as well as wines; a café with a gorgeous terrace that overlooks the vineyard is open for good coffee, delicious cream teas and simple but very tasty lunches.

## DEVIL'S HOLE

From the Priory Inn car park just north of La Mare, a footpath leads down to the cliffs and Le Creux de Vis (Screw Hole) or, as it's more familiarly known, **Devil's Hole** ㉔. From

### Puffins at Plémont

The burrows in the cliffs at Plémont have been the nesting site of a small colony of puffins for more than a century. From around 1,000 pairs in the 1950s the number has now dwindled to just a dozen. Climate change and food shortages, particularly the declining number of sand eels, are thought to be the causes. You will only be able to spot the puffins if you come in spring when they are nesting.

*Gate detail at La Mare Wine Estate*

a narrow causeway you can watch the waves crash dramatically into a yawning chasm in the cliff as the tides come up. This blowhole was created by the sea eroding the roof of what was once a cave. The dramatic name of Devil's Hole was acquired in the 19th century and is believed to have originated from the shipwreck of a French boat in 1851. The figurehead of the vessel was discovered in the hole here, and a local sculptor transformed it into a wooden devil with horns. A replica of the original towers over the pond beside the path that winds down to the Devil's Hole.

## BONNE NUIT

Sheltering below the heather-clad cliffs, the next bay is picturesque **Bonne Nuit** ㉕ (Good Night). The name was recorded back in the 12th century, refuting the long-held belief that it derived from King Charles II's parting words *Bonne nuit, belle Jersey*, when he left from the port here after his exile on the island. The name probably referred to the shelter that the little harbour offered to sailors overnight.

The unspoilt bay comprises little more than a stone jetty sheltering the harbour; a sand, shingle and rock beach taken up by little fishing boats that go out daily for lobsters and crabs; and the popular **Bonne Nuit Beach Café** with lovely views of the bay. A familiar sight at low or mid tide is the gaggle of ducks waddling across the beach, hopeful of a crumb from the cream teas served up by the café.

On the rugged headland east of the bay the British-built **La Crête Fort** (1830) used to be a weekend retreat for the island's lieutenant-governor. Now anyone can holiday here through Jersey Heritage. There are a couple of simply-furnished bedrooms, wonderful views over open seas to Guernsey, Sark and the coast of France, and a secluded walled garden where you can sit and contemplate the sunset.

## BOULEY BAY

Two other historic forts, built in the line of defence against the French, have been converted for holiday lets at **Bouley Bay** ㉖ to the southeast. Fort Leicester (named after Queen Elizabeth I's Earl of Leicester) sleeps up to eight. The more basic L'Etacquerel Fort has 'stone hut' accommodation for 30 people – and space for up to 60 by day. Accessed via a steep coastal path, and a high wooden bridge over the moat, this is a peaceful atmospheric spot for a back-to-basics gathering. There are no utilities (prepare yourselves for composting toilets only) and you will need to bring your own sleeping bags.

Bouley Bay consists of no more than a steeply shelving pebble-and-rock beach (voted one of the cleanest in the UK), the Water's Edge Apartments  and a diving school. With its deep, clear and pond-like waters, this is the main place on Jersey for scuba diving. It's also a good spot for kayaking, swimming and snorkelling – or just sitting at **Mad Mary's Café** right on the beach and enjoying the views. Bouley Bay is the venue for the British Hill Climb Championships, and three times a year the peace of the bay is shattered as saloon cars, racing cars, sports cars and motor bikes tear up the steep hill.

## ROZEL

Nestling below wooded slopes, **Rozel** ㉗ is a romantic little creek, with a handful of fishermen's cottages, a small port and shingle beach. There has always been a fishing harbour here, and in the 1820s it was the base for around 30 oyster-fishing boats. Today fishermen go out for lobster and crab (the Hungry Man kiosk by the pier serves a great crab sandwich and a 90p mug of tea). Behind the bay barracks were built in 1810 but the anticipated attack on Rozel never took place – despite it being the closest point on the island to France. The barracks have been converted into a luxury private home.

Behind the bay the **Vallée de Rozel** is lush and verdant, planted with subtropical trees and shrubs. Tucked away in the valley is the elegant **Château La Chaire Hotel** (see page 133) with over 8

L'Etacquerel Fort at sunset

acres (3 hectares) of beautiful gardens and grounds, created by Samuel Curtis, a 19th-century botanist and former director of Kew Gardens. Curtis first saw the site in 1841 and, having searched all over the British Isles, instantly knew that this steep-sided valley, with a stream running onto the shingle beach of Rozel Bay, was the ideal spot for his subtropical plant paradise. He built a small house here under the cliffs and created a series of paths and ter-

### Fearsome hound

Jersey abounds with myth and superstition. On the north coast tales used to spread of the Black Dog of Bouley Bay, a terrifying beast with huge teeth and eyes the size of saucers that roamed the coastline. The tales were probably invented by smugglers hoping to scare away parishioners from the coast while they landed their cargoes of brandy and tobacco.

races. The house was pulled down at the end of the century, and a grander one took its place (now the hotel). During the Occupation the Germans dug up some of the prized trees, and today few of Curtis' original species survive.

## JERSEY ZOO

'The world is as delicate and as complicated as a spider's web. If you touch one thread you send shudders running through all the other threads. We are not just touching the webs, we are tearing great holes in it…' *Gerald Durrell (author and naturalist)*.

Gerald Durrell's first intelligible word is said to have been 'zoo'. From the age of six he had wanted to create a safe place for his collection of animals. In 1959, 34 years later, he realised his childhood dream by creating Jersey Zoo. It was set up not as a zoo in the conventional sense but as a sanctuary and breeding centre for some

*Rozel harbour*

of the world's most endangered animal species. Durrell's objectives were to provide a safe haven for these rare species, build up colonies, then send them to organisations worldwide, who would return them to the wild and reintroduce them to areas where they had become extinct.

Durrell chose the dodo as symbol of the zoo, thereby demonstrating his commitment to saving rare species from the fate that befell the flightless bird from Mauritius. The zoo is operated by the **Durrell Wildlife Conservation Trust** ㉘ (www.durrell.org; daily 9.30am–6pm, until 5pm off-season; bus Nos 3, 13 and 23). Since 1977 conservationists from around the world have been trained in the theory and practice of endangered species recovery, and the trust has earned a worldwide reputation for pioneering conservation techniques. Durrell died in 1995 and is survived by his widow, zoologist Dr Lee Durrell, who continues his dedicated work at the trust.

Conservation mainly focuses on the island areas of the Galápagos, the Caribbean islands, Madagascar and Indian Ocean islands and India – but not forgetting Jersey's own dwindling amphibians such as the agile frog and the common toad (or *crapaud*), the island's beloved mascot. Among the species that have been pulled back from the brink are the pink pigeons and kestrels from Mauritius, the St Lucia whiptail, the thick-billed parrots from Arizona, and the pygmy hog, the world's oldest and rarest pig, which has been successfully reintroduced to the wildlife sanctuary in Assam, northeast India. In the late 1980s a couple of St Lucia parrots flew back to the Caribbean with British Airways, accompanied by the prime minister of St Lucia who had come to Jersey specifically to escort them home. Recent projects include the Jamaican boa or yellowsnake, the Madagascan teal and flat-tailed tortoise,

*Flamingos at Jersey Zoo*

the Floreana mocking bird from the Galápagos and the Montserrat mountain chicken, which is in fact a large frog, tasting of chicken. The latter is endangered by a deadly fungal disease discovered on the Carribean island.

If you're expecting unhappy animals cramped in cages you're in for a pleasant surprise. The setting is a 32-acre (13 hectare) oasis of woodland, landscaped lawns and water gardens, surrounding an 18th-century granite manor house. Wherever possible the trust has tried to cultivate the native habitat for family groups of the endangered species. Certainly by average zoo standards, the animals do look remarkably content. The golden-headed lion tamarins roam in the woods, the gorillas play in a spacious compound, flamingos

## GERALD DURRELL

Gerald Durrell was born in India and from an early age collected 'everything from minnows to woodlice'. After the death of his father, when Gerald was only 3 years old, his mother brought him and his sister to England to be educated. Durrell detested school, left at the age of 9, and was educated by private tutors who concentrated on what he loved: natural history. Four idyllic years from the age of 10 were spent in Corfu, surrounded by a menagerie of animals. This led to his best-known novel, *My Family and Other Animals* (1956), which has sold five million copies. The hit TV series, The Durrells (2016––2019) was based on Durrell's three autobiographical books about his early years living in Corfu. At the age of 21 he inherited £3,000, which funded his first animal-collecting expedition – to the British Cameroons – and he spent the next decade collecting animals for British zoos. Durrell wrote 33 books, hosted TV series and radio programmes and won nine international awards for leadership in conservation.

wade in the lake, reptiles have their own tropical habitat-simulated quarters, aye-ayes have a special nocturnal unit, and orangutans swing from ropes or stick twigs in logs to prise out the honey.

Among the favourite residents are the silver-back lowland gorillas, Mapema and Ya Pli, descended from Jambo, the 'gentle giant' who hit the headlines in 1986 when he protected a 5-year-old boy who fell into

*One of Jersey Zoo's silver-back lowland gorillas*

the compound. Jambo, who died in 1992, was the first male gorilla to be reared in captivity.

## THE EAST COAST

Star attractions of the east coast are Mont Orgueil Castle, a majestic fortress that played a pivotal role in the island's history, and the picturesque port of Gorey, which shelters beneath its walls. From here the Royal Bay of Grouville, sheltered from westerly winds, stretches southwards for nearly 2 miles (3km). Queen Victoria was so impressed by the spacious, sandy bay that she added the royal prefix after her visit in 1859.

## ST CATHERINE'S BREAKWATER

The most significant feature of **St Catherine's Bay** is the massive **breakwater** ㉙ which encloses it on the northern side. In

Red ruffed lemur at Jersey Zoo

response to coastal installations, which the French had created at Cherbourg, the British decided to build a naval base with a large deepwater harbour at St Catherine's. Warnings that the waters were too shallow for warships went unheeded and in 1847 breakwaters were built both here and at Archirondel Tower to the south. By the time the St Catherine's breakwater was complete, eight years on, the British realised their blunder and the project was abandoned. Today the breakwater provides a bracing half-mile (0.8km) walk, a shelter for dinghies and a useful pier for anglers. From the lighthouse at the end there are fine views of the coast to the south, the small pebble and rock bay of Fliquet to the north, which you can reach on foot, and the rocky islets known as **Les Écréhous** (see box). On a clear day you can see as far as the Normandy coast.

Just south of the breakwater a **German bunker** houses tanks of around 6,500 turbot, ranging from tiddlers to mature 2.5lb (1kg) fish. The larger ones are sold to restaurateurs, fishmongers and the public. There are guided tours every Sunday in season or possible with 24 hours' notice (tel: 01534 868836).

From St Catherine's Bay you can walk all the way to Gorey – or drive on the coastal B29. A distinctive landmark is the red and white **Archirondel Tower** ㉚ on the eponymous beach, built in 1792 as a garrison for artillery soldiers. The tower has been restored and is now available for 'stone hut' holiday accommodation. Inland, a walk through **St Catherine's Wood** provides a delightful shady diversion from the coast.

## GEOFFREY'S LEAP

The rocky promontory between Anne Port Bay and Gorey Harbour is known as Le Saut Geoffroi or **Geoffrey's Leap**, after a popular

### KINGS OF LES ÉCRÉHOUS

The reef of rocks lying mid-way between Jersey and Normandy, known as Les Écréhous, has been part of Jersey's bailiwick since 1953. The reef expands by about 80 percent at low tide and it's a lovely spot to visit on a boat trip in season. A couple of 'kings' have inhabited the reef: in 1848 Phillipe Pinel lived with his wife on Blanche Île for 46 years and was proclaimed 'king' by local fishermen who lived in the huts here. In the 1960s Alphonse Le Gastelois, an eccentric fisherman and farmhand who was suspected of being the mystery child attacker known as 'the beast of Jersey', moved to Les Écréhous and lived alone here for 14 years, claiming that the island belonged to him. (By the time he returned to Jersey, the real beast, one Edward Paisnel, had been tracked down, convicted of 13 counts of assault, rape and sodomy and sentenced to 30 years' imprisonment).

Jersey legend. A renowned womaniser, Geoffrey was convicted of sexual harassment and sentenced to be thrown off the cliffs here on to the rocks below. Miraculously he missed the rocks and surfaced at Anne Port to the north. The reaction among islanders was divided: some wanted him thrown off the cliffs again, others, including some female admirers, saw his survival as proof of innocence. Seeing another opportunity to impress local women, Geoffrey took it upon himself to repeat the leap – but this time he hurled himself to destruction.

Off a country lane inland from Geoffrey's Leap and approached along a leafy path is **La Pouquelaye de Faldouet** ㉛ , an impressive and somewhat elusive 50ft (15m) long neolithic passage grave. Dolmens like these played an important role in the rich folklore of the island, and this one, tucked away off a rural lane,

*Anne Port, in the south of St Catherine's Bay*

*Mont Orgueil Castle*

retains an air of mysterious antiquity. Look on any Jersey 10p coin and you will see a picture of it.

## MONT ORGUEIL CASTLE

Even if you have never visited **Mont Orgueil Castle** ❸❷ (Jan Sat 10am–4pm, Feb–mid-Mar & Nov–mid-Dec Fri–Mon 10am–4pm, mid-Mar–Oct daily 10am–6pm), it is likely to look familiar. Symbolic of Jersey, the photogenic fortress is reproduced on countless post-cards, holiday brochures and guides. Commanding a spectacular promontory above the harbour, built into the granite rocks, it makes a wonderful backdrop to Gorey Harbour, both by day and by night when the battlements are floodlit.

The earliest fortifications date back to the very early 13th century when King John had lost control of Normandy and the island needed protection against the threat of French invasion. Built in a concentric series of defences, the castle proved to be an impregnable fortress.

As warfare changed the fortification was expanded and strengthened. Fifteen French attacks were made between 1204 and 1600, most of them unsuccessful. One notable exception was the French invasion of 1468 which resulted in a seven-year occupation.

Mont Orgueil was essentially a bow-and-arrow castle and by the late 16th century it was no longer able to sustain modern warfare. Elizabeth Castle, equipped with cannons, was built on Jersey's south coast. Mont Orgueil would have been razed to the ground were it not for the intervention of Sir Walter Raleigh, then governor of the island, who decided that the stately fort should stay. It became a prison in the 17th century, then in 1789 a refuge for aristocrats fleeing the reign of terror and the guillotine in France. In 1907 the castle was finally given by the Crown to the States of Jersey and in 1996 Queen Elizabeth II handed it over to the islanders.

A network of ancient, dark staircases and cobbled passageways lead up to lofty ramparts. At the top Somerset Tower, adapted under the German Occupation as an observation post, commands magnificent 360-degree views of the island and across to France. Within the castle there is plenty to explore in the way of medieval keeps, cellars, towers, chapels and gun platforms. History is kept alive with audio-visual presentations, large artworks (such as the gruesome carving showing the fate that might await those defending the castle from attack), twice-weekly hawking demonstrations and occasional tales and displays of Tudor life. The castle also makes a perfect backdrop for occasional medieval drama and re-enactments.

## GOREY

Below the castle walls **Gorey Harbour** is a picture postcard ensemble of quaint houses, pubs and seafood cafés, clustering around a harbour of fishing boats, yachts and pleasure craft. In the early 19th century the port grew prosperous on the oyster trade, becoming known as 'the pearl of the east'. The British muscled in on the lucrative industry and by the 1830s there were around 260 oyster vessels and 1,400 fishermen – along with 600–700 women and children who gave a helping hand. Fishing cottages were built at Gorey and a pier to protect the oyster fleet, but the fishermen became overambitious and by the 1860s the oyster beds were almost exhausted. The village returned to its shellfish-producing traditions by introducing oyster and mussel farms in the last century. Up to 600 tonnes of oysters are now produced annually – and not surprisingly, they feature on virtually every Gorey menu. At very low tide you can see the oyster beds in Grouville Bay, and, more prominent, the rows of wooden poles where the Bouchot mussels grow.

## THE ROYAL BAY OF GROUVILLE

The huge expanse of sands stretching south from Gorey Harbour, known as the **Royal Bay of Grouville** ㉝, attracts water sports

*Gorey Harbour*

aficionados, joggers, sunbathers and swimmers. Bathing is safe but with the huge tidal movement you should be prepared for quite a walk out to sea. In July and August, Gorey Watersports organises kayaking, water-skiing, wakeboarding, speedboat trips and banana rides – wetsuits, life-jackets and tuition are all provided.

During World War II the Germans used a million tonnes of Grouville sand to construct the concrete fortifications around the coast. The spacious Grouville Common that borders the beach saw duels fought in the 18th century, and horse racing in Victorian times. If you're strolling on the common watch out for stray golf balls. This is home to the exclusive Royal Jersey Golf Club, where Grouville-born Harry Vardon (six times British Open Championship winner) trained in the early years. Vardon was the first professional golfer to play in knickerbockers and is famous for the overlapping grip which bears his name and

The Seymour Tower at low tide

which is used by the vast majority of golfers. The club has been here since 1878 and remained unchanged until the German Occupation when the links were transformed into a minefield. Today the club is the most exclusive on the island. Visitors are welcome provided they are members of a recognised golf club.

This whole stretch of coast, from St Helier Harbour to Gorey Pier, is a protected site, characterised by weather-worn reefs, mud, sand and shingle shores and exposed twice a day by one of the largest tidal ranges in the world.

## SEYMOUR TOWER

The predominantly rocky shoreline to the south of Grouville Bay is guarded by a series of towers, built in the 18th century but never actually used to defend the island. Some of the towers have been turned into private residences. At the southeastern tip **La Rocque Harbour** was the arrival point of Baron de Rullecourt and his troops, who made a surprise night-time landing in 1781, only to be defeated in the Battle of Jersey. At low tide you can walk out to Seymour Tower, isolated on a rocky islet 2 miles (3km) off La Rocque Point. The walk takes you over an eerie wilderness of gullies, sandbars, reefs and rocks and the low-lying coast provides a rich breeding ground for thousands of wintering waders, gulls and wildfowl. Watch out for the tides – the sea comes galloping in at a frighteningly fast rate.

Those with a sense of adventure might like to stay overnight in **Seymour Tower** ❸, which can accommodate up to seven guests, sleeping in bunk beds. There are no luxuries like running water but drinking water is provided, as are logs for the wood-burning stove. You carry your own food, clothes and sleeping bags out to the tower. The only hitch, at least for independently minded visitors, is that you must be accompanied by a Seymour Tower Guide who guides you to and from the tower and stays the night. (For further information, go to www.jerseyheritage.org).

Jersey is a water sports paradise

# THINGS TO DO

## SPORTS

Big surfing beaches, rock-bound coves, clear diving waters and gently shelving sands make for a wide range of aquatic activities. Traditional sports, such as sailing, surfing and water-skiing, have been joined in by new adrenalin-fuelled activities such as blokarting, skydiving, abseiling, coasteering and kiteboarding. Add to these boat trips, fishing, five golf courses, stylish spas and gyms, and there's enough action for any sports and fitness enthusiast. There are around 20 sports and activity operators on the island. For the full picture check the Jersey Tourism website: www.jersey.com.

### WATER SPORTS

**Surfing.** With towering Atlantic rollers and a huge beach, St Ouen's bay on the west coast, is *the* place to surf. The Jersey Surfboard Club, one of the oldest in Europe, established in 1959, celebrated its 50th anniversary in 2009 with the European Surfing Championships. Surf schools can arrange equipment hire and give you advice on how to ride the rollers. Jersey Surf School (www.jerseysurfschool.co.uk) at the Watersplash offers professional surf coaching by accredited instructors and a full range of equipment for hire. Unless you're a real pro, keep to the areas between the yellow and red flags, which are surveyed by lifeguards. Bodyboarding and windsurfing equipment are also available, though beginner windsurfers are better off at St Brelade's, St Aubin's or Grouville where the waters are calmer. High-octane thrill-seekers can try kitesurfing, where you use a surfboard and large kite to propel yourself at high speed across the ocean. To get safely up and running on a kitesurf takes around three two-hour sessions over the

*Heading out into the surf at St Ouen's Bay*

course of a few days. The location depends on which way the wind is blowing.

**Wakeboarding and Water-skiing.** The fast-growing sport of wakeboarding is likened to snow-boarding on water, with a speedboat pulling you through the waves. You can try it out at St Brelade's Bay, St Aubin's Bay and the Royal Bay of Grouville. The best spots for water-skiing are St Aubin's Bay and Grouville, where the waters are not too choppy.

**Sailing.** Marinas and harbours have excellent facilities for sailors but beginners should beware of sunken reefs, big tides and strong currents. Experienced sailors can charter boats or join local regattas. Flexible day or evening sailing trips, focusing on the waters around Jersey, are organised by **Jersey Yachting** (tel: 07797 792858, www.jerseyyachting.co.uk), who sail from St Helier. The catamaran can be chartered, and individuals or couples can often share trips with others; if not, it works out very expensive.

**Sea kayaking/Coasteering.** Jersey's clear waters, remote coves and rich marine life make for excellent kayaking and coasteering (scrambling around the rocks, cliff jumping and swimming through caves). Kayaks can be hired at the main beaches. The kayak specialists are Jersey Kayak Adventures (www.jersey-kayakadventures.co.uk) who operate from venues all over the island. Tours are suitable for all ages and abilities, and all equipment is provided.

## Blokarting

It's not only adrenalin junkies who practise this fast and furious sport. It doesn't take long to grasp the basics and you don't have to go at 55mph (88kmph), the maximum speed. The blokart, a three-wheeled kart with a large sail, propels you along the beach. You steer the cart with one hand, and control the speed with the other.

**Diving.** Bouley Bay, with its clear, calm waters, is the most popular part of the island for scuba diving. The Bouley Bay Dive Centre (www.scubadivingjersey.com), which is over 50 years old and welcomes beginners and experts alike. Divers with experience can dive down to wrecks of ships sunk in World War II and other vessels that have been deliberately scuttled to provide shelter for marine life.

**Swimming.** If you don't mind cool water, Jersey can be idyllic for swimming. Sea temperatures average around 17°C (63°F) in summer, which deters most beachgoers and, once past the paddlers, you can have huge expanses of clear seawater all to yourself. Beware, however, of heavy swells and swimming on incoming tides. Lifeguards patrol St Ouen's beach, St Brelade's Bay, Plémont and some of the other main beaches from mid-May to the end of September. The patrolled areas are indicated by red and yellow flags. Red flags indicate that sea conditions are dangerous.

### The Polar Bears

The seawater swimming enthusiasts known as 'The Polar Bears' meet at Havre des Pas Bathing Pool for daily swims throughout summer, and weekly ones in winter. These Jersey residents welcome visitors to join them. Depending on the sea temperature it might be a quick dip or a mile-long swim around the bay (tel: 01534 728 782).

**Fishing.** There is still plenty of marine life around the Jersey shores. From rocks, breakwaters and harbours, anglers can fish for black bream, mullet, bass, wrasse and conger. Low tide is the best time for fishing for crabs, prawns and devil fish in the rock pools. For boat fishing trips from St Helier consult the official Jersey website: www.jersey. com.

**Boat Trips.** Cruising around the gorgeous Jersey coast, racing a catamaran, spotting dolphins or seals or taking a ferry to France are all among the boating options. For visiting offshore reefs and seeing wildlife from RIBs contact Jersey Safaris at www. jerseyseafaris.com. Standard cruise trips in a catamaran along 15 miles (24km) of the south coast depart daily in season from Albert Quay, St Helier.

## LAND SPORTS

**Golf.** Jersey has half a dozen golf courses and an impressive pedigree. Harry Vardon, six-times winner of the British Open, was born here, and Ian Woosnam is an island resident. Proof of handicap is required at the 18-hole championship courses: **La Moye** at La Route Orange, St Brelade, tel: 01534 743401, www.lamoyegolfclub. co.uk and **Royal Jersey Golf Club**, La Chemin au Grèves, Grouville, tel: 01534 854416, www.royaljersey.com. Anyone can play at the 18-hole course at **Les Mielles**, St Ouen's Bay, tel: 01534 482787, www.lesmielles.com, or the 9-hole courses at Wheatlands, off Le

Vieux Beaumont, St Peter, tel: 01534 888877, www. wheatlandsjersey.com and **Les Ormes Leisure Village**, St Brelade, tel: 01534 497000, www.lesormesjersey.co.uk.

The Fort Regent leisure centre has a large, well-equipped gym, badminton, children's soft play and other activities; **Les Quennevais Sports Centre** close to St Brelade's Bay (tel: 01534 449880) offers tennis, a 25m swimming pool, gym and other indoor sports.

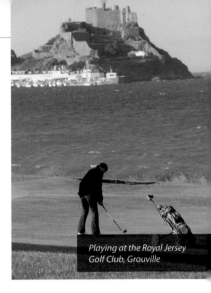

*Playing at the Royal Jersey Golf Club, Grouville*

## OTHER ACTIVITIES

### SPAS, HEALTH AND LEISURE

For an island traditionally associated with old-fashioned seaside holidays, Jersey has certainly made a splash when it comes to spas. In St Helier alone there are five hotels with state-of-the-art spas where you can choose from a range of treatments, use the indoor pools and high-tech gyms. At the **Spa Sirène** in the Royal Yacht Hotel you can unwind with a steam mud *rasul*, sauna, or hydrotherapy bath, and chill out in the indoor vitality pool or under ice-cold bucket showers. Hotel de France's **Ayush Wellness Spa** is based on ancient Hindu health and healing principles, while the chic **Club Hotel & Spa** has a swish spa that offers all kinds

There are plenty of lovely walks to be had in Jersey

of feel-good treatments. At the Grand Jersey Hotel's luxury **Grand Spa**, guests and residents are pampered in six treatment rooms and at St Brelade's, the spa at the **L'Horizon Hotel** overlooks the beautiful bay.

For a cheaper health option to the hotel spas try **Fitness First** at St Helier's Waterfront Centre (www.fitnessfirstjersey.com) with a gym, cardio theatre, spinning room, sauna, steam room and beauty room. The neighbouring **Aqua Splash** (www.aquasplash.je) on the Waterfront Centre has an 80ft (25m) six-lane pool, and an outdoor pool with flumes and slides.

## WALKING

Jersey packs in plenty of walks, from gentle strolls along seafront promenades, or down leafy lanes through woodland valleys, to the more dramatic north coast cliffs. In addition to the footpaths there are 50 miles (80km) of Green Lanes, with a speed limit of 15 mph (24 kmph) giving priority to pedestrians, cyclists and horse riders.

Escorted walks take place almost every day from April to September and themes cover all aspects of the island, including wildlife, local customs, maritime history, smuggling and the German Occupation. Tours are led by enthusiastic and knowledgeable guides and the fees are very affordable. More expensive, but well worth it, are the occasional 'Moonwalks', at low tide only, across the lunar-like landscape to Seymour Tower or Icho Tower on the southeast coast. The tides can be treacherous here, and going alone is not advised. You can also visit the oyster and mussel beds off La Rocque Harbour, learn about their cultivation then sample oysters at the local pub. The Jersey Tourism website (www.jersey.com/walking-in-jersey) has details of self-guided walks, with information on length and time, degree of difficulty, transport, attractions en route and refreshment stops. Their free walking guide can be picked up at the tourist office or downloaded from the website. Jersey Walk Adventures (www.jerseywalkadventures.co.uk) offer guided walks with a variety of themes, among them Seaweed Foraging, Oyster Trails and Bioluminescence on the Beach (an evening walk revealing glow-in-the-dark fireflies or worms).

## BIKING

Fit cyclists can forget the car on Jersey and use pedal power to enjoy the scenery. No distance is too far to cycle – though the hills can be strenuous and on occasions the local 4x4s leave you little space on the narrow country lanes. Cyclists should plan their routes around the 60-mile (96km) signposted cycle network, including 50 miles (80km) of Green Lanes, which carry a 15mph (24kmph) speed limit for cars (usually, but not always, adhered to). Jersey Tourism provides a free map detailing cycling routes and the website gives details for self-guided bike tours. One of the easiest and most attractive routes, suitable for families with small children, is the designated footpath/cycle ride following the old railway line from St Aubin to Corbière (for bike hire, see page 115).

# BUSH CAMPS

Discover wild edible and medicinal plants, cook on a beach fire, learn natural navigating skills, make cordage using plants and

## WALKS AND STROLLS

The North Coast is the best place for walking. The **North Coast Footpath** runs for 15 miles (24km) from **Grosnez** to **Rozel**. Some sections are quite steep, particularly as the path climbs up from the bays, but there is nothing seriously challenging. The walk can either be done in its entirety over a very long day, or in separate, relatively short, sections at a gentler pace. The scenery is best in spring when wild flowers are in full bloom and birds come ashore to nest. The path occasionally diverts from the coast, but the route is well signed. Getting there and back is best done by bus. No. 3 goes from St Helier to Rozel, No. 8 returns from Grosnez. One of the most spectacular stretches is Bonne Nuit to Bouley Bay (4 miles/2.5km, served by No. 4 bus from St Helier). You could also walk west from Bonne Nuit to La Saline. Check the Jersey bus timetable on www.libertybus.je.

Walks in the southwest corner of the island afford some splendid coastal views. **Portelet Common** on the headland between Portelet Bay and Ouaisné Bay commands a stunning panorama over Ouaisné and St Brelade's Bay to the northwest, and over Portelet Bay to the east. **Noirmont Promontory** is not quite as scenic but provides pleasant clifftop strolls and historic interest in its German Occupation relics. A longer walk takes you all the way from **Ouaisné Bay** to **La Corbière** (you could also start at St Brelade's or Beauport). Features such as the island prison and desalination plant don't enhance the scenery and the track occasionally diverts inland, but most of this rugged cliff path is unspoilt, with superb sea views. The walk ends with the striking view of Corbière Lighthouse (see page 55). From **St Helier** to **St Aubin** the long seafront promenade makes an ideal leisurely stroll or cycle ride; from St Aubin you can continue to Corbière along the old railway route, now a peaceful cycle- and footpath through varied scenery, from red squirrel-inhabited woodland to gorse-clad heathland. It's a gentle climb of 4 miles (6.4km), and you can return to St Aubin or St Helier by bus No.12a.

trees and construct your own shelter. Activities at Wild Adventures include rock climbing, coasteering, abseiling, boogie-boarding and cycle tours as well as 6-day survival courses. Accommodation is offered in yurts. For more information contact Kazz at Wild Adventures (www.wildadventuresjersey.com, tel: 07797-886242).

## ARTS AND ENTERTAINMENT

Most of the entertainment is focused on St Helier. **The Jersey Arts Centre**, Phillips Street, St Helier (tel: 01534 700444, www.artscentre.je) is a non-profit-making organisation that stages contemporary and classical concerts plus theatre and art exhibitions. The **Jersey Opera House** in Gloucester Street (tel: 01534 511115, www.jerseyoperahouse.co.uk) has been beautifully

*Jersey Opera House*

restored and stages musical extravaganzas, concerts, drama, dance and very occasional operas. Fort Regent (www.gov.je/events) hosts occasional classical and popular concerts, exhibitions and fairs.

## BARS, PUBS AND CLUBS

Jersey is not renowned for nightlife but there are a handful of late-night venues in central St Helier and plenty of friendly pubs throughout the island. Regarded by affluent young financiers as one of the coolest bars is **The Drift**, Royal Yacht Hotel, Liberation Square, a popular after-work rendezvous and a late-night bar offering a huge range of cocktails, drinks and snacks, live music or DJs. Stylish **Libertys** (www.libertysjersey.co.uk) at Liberty Wharf has terraces overlooking the marina and comprises the **Quayside Bistro and Grill**, specialising in fresh fish and the **Vittoria** bar and nightclub. The adjoining **Fox and Firkin** is a traditional bar with a good selection of real ale and beers, and a big screen TV for sporting events. With Jersey's biggest screen, this is also the place to head if you're planning to watch a big game. For details of concerts, live bands or DJs, pick up a copy of the *Jersey Evening Post*.

## SHOPPING

Jersey is not a full member of the EU, and VAT is non-existent. However, this doesn't mean that the shops are packed with bargains. Many of them put up prices for 'freight surcharge', then add to this the 5 percent Goods and Services tax, and the prices are around the same as those in the UK. Moreover, not all goods are VAT free – some shops retain VAT on goods that have come from the UK. The best buys are wines, spirits and tobacco and, to a lesser extent, cosmetics, perfume and jewellery, which are all duty free.

For customs restrictions that apply to luxury goods purchased in the Channel Islands, see page 128.

The main shopping centre is St Helier, which has a pleasant pedestrianised High Street with the usual chain stores, plus department stores, gift shops and a large number of jewellers and shops selling cosmetics. As well as browsing here don't miss the indoor **Central Market,** a Victorian gem packed with stalls selling everything from fruit and veg to antiques and jewellery, nor the **Fish Market** to see the catch of the day (see page 32 for the markets).

*Cigarette packet dogs at St Aubin's Harbour Gallery*

**Liberty Wharf** on the waterfront is a covered shopping mall converted from Victorian granite warehouses. It has a mix of UK chain stores and Jersey boutiques, with plenty of cafés.

## ISLAND ARTS AND CRAFTS

**Jersey Pottery** (www.jerseypottery.com) is renowned for ceramics These can be bought at their shop at 43 Halkett Place, St Helier, at their concession in De Gruchy's department store nearby in King Street, at Jersey airport and in 700 other outlets in 30 countries. The pottery is now made in the UK, Europe and other countries. Catering is now a major part of the business, and Jersey Pottery cafés and restaurants, renowned for good quality and service, can be found at St Helier, Gorey and St Brelade's Bay (see page 106).

Some of the most popular shopping outlets are attached to craft centres, spread across the island. The **Harbour Gallery** at Le Boulevard, St Aubin (daily 10am–5pm) is a large, well-run arts and crafts centre, with regularly changing contemporary exhibitions and some innovative paintings, textiles, sculpture and designer fashion by over 80 local artists. There's an excellent little café here too.

At **Jersey Pearl** at St Ouen (www.jerseypearl.com) you can have your own necklace made or choose from an extensive range of cultured, freshwater or simulated pearls. **Catherine Best** at Les Chenolles, St Peter (www.catherinebest.com), who is based in a lovely old windmill, creates innovative pieces of jewellery, often from rare, fabulously coloured gemstones. For less expensive souvenirs try **Jersey Lavender** inland from St Brelade's Bay (see page

*Fun among the rock pools at Ouaisné Bay*

53), where soaps, oils, colognes, creams and candles are made from the lavender essence.

Locally made wines and spirits, black butter (see page 103), jams and jellies can be found at **La Mare Wine Estate** in St Mary (see page 65), which also has a shop, Maison La Mare, in King Street, St Helier. For other Jersey specialities look for the red logo of Genuine Jersey, which promotes local produce. This covers crafts and jewellery as well as food and drink.

## CHILDREN'S JERSEY

For a traditional family holiday, Jersey has the ideal ingredients: acres of sandy beaches, crab-filled rock pools, numerous sporting activities and a variety of family attractions. Top of the list should be **Jersey Zoo** (see page 69), whose gorillas, orangutans, fruit bats and other endangered species will keep youngsters entertained (and educated) for at least half a day. Farmyard animals are one of the attractions at Hamptonne Country Life Museum (see page 40). In St Helier the **Maritime Museum** (see page 34) is full of hands-on exhibits, and the amphibious castle ferry to Elizabeth Castle (see page 36) makes an entertaining excursion. The **aMaizin! Adventure Park** (La Hougue Farm, St Peter, tel: 01534 482116, www.jerseyleisure.com) is one of the most popular family outings with barnyard animals and a whole range of outdoor and indoor activities including gold panning, a giant jumping pillow, tractor rides (Easter–September) and go-karting. All activities are included in the entrance free. The maze itself – a labyrinth constructed entirely of maize – opens in July and closes at the end of September. The **Valley Activity Centre** at Les Ormes Leisure Club, St Brelade (www.valleyadventure.je) is ideal for older children – and adults. The attractive valley here is the setting for a range of exciting activities, from zip wires, aerial trekking and

Powerfan freefall (jumping from a 40ft (12m) tower), to a military-style assault course, paintballing and orienteering.

The **Pallot Steam, Motor and General Museum** in Trinity (www.pallotmuseum.co.uk) is a fascinating collection of steam and farm machinery, motor vehicles, vintage bikes and organs, put together by the late Don Pallot, a talented Jersey engineer. He invented farming implements to facilitate life for Jersey farmers, among them the Pallot Elevator Digger and the Last Furrow Reversible Plough.

The best beach for youngsters is **St Brelade's Bay**, with its great swathe of gently sloping sands and shallow waters, bucket-and-spade shops and child-friendly cafés. Children who are used to warm swimming pools may find the sea water on the cool side but it's never too cold for paddling or splashing around in the shallows. The neighbouring **Ouaisné Bay** has some great rock pools at the far end where children can mess around fishing for shrimps, crabs and devil fish. Older children who are strong swimmers will love bodyboarding on the wind-swept bay of St Ouen's – or just sitting at a beachside café watching the stand-up surfers catching the Atlantic rollers. On a rainy day take children to **Aqua Splash** at St Helier's Waterfront Centre, which has an indoor pool with wave machine and bubble pool – plus an outdoor one with flumes and a tyre ride.

*The Pallot steam museum*

# CALENDAR OF EVENTS

For a full listing of festivals and events happening in Jersey, go to www.jersey.com/events or pick up a current copy of the *What's On* guide for the events of the month.

**May:** *Liberation Day* (9 May): celebrating the liberation from German Occupying forces during World War II. Towards the end of May the *Jersey Food Festival* celebrates the best from local food producers, chefs and artisans.

**June:** *June in Bloom* floral festival: 4 days towards the end of June that feature open gardens, demonstrations, flower shows, workshops and walks; the Collas Crill Island Walk (www.collascrill.com), a 48-mile (77-km) walk for charity.

**July:** *Jersey Folklore Festival* in People's Park.

**August:** *Battle of Flowers* (second Thursday in August): A highlight in the Jersey calendar, featuring a spectacular parade of flower-decked floats, musicians and entertainers, headed by Miss Jersey and a celebrity Mr Battle. Parishes make their own floats and competition between them is fierce. The Friday evening sees the *Moonlight Parade* of flower-covered floats. *Gorey Fête* in mid-August is a day of beach events, games, stalls, fairground rides and music.

**September:** The *Jersey International Air Display*, an immensely popular event that has been running annually for 62 years and is one of the biggest free airshows in the British Isles and *The Weekender Festival*, which aims to bring Jersey together to mark the end of every summer with good music and food.

**October:** Autumn events include the *Royal Jersey Horticultural Show* and *La Faîs'sie d'Cidre*, the lively Cider Festival at Hamptonne Country Life Museum.

**October–November:** Restaurants are packed out during the *Tennerfest*, six weeks (Oct–mid-Nov) when fixed menus start at £10 at over 100 restaurants.

**December:** *La Fête de Noué*, a Christmas festival, with street entertainment, parades and markets in St Helier.

# FOOD AND DRINK

Eating out is an important part of life on the island and Jersey residents are spoilt for choice. A vast array of fabulously fresh seafood and fish is caught around the shores, and that's not the only local produce. Jersey produces its own vegetables, fruits, herbs, beef, pork and even cheeses. Not to mention the famous Jersey Royal potatoes and the creamy milk from Jersey cows.

Prosperous financiers and tax exiles ensure a year-round clientele at up-market restaurants; but at the other end of the spectrum there are plenty of more humble eateries, from country pubs and fish and chip outlets to beach cafés and kiosks. Seafood features in some capacity on virtually every menu. It might be a platter of lobster, scallops, crab and prawns, a succulent sea bass or bream, or just a tasty crab sandwich at a seaside kiosk.

Given the proximity to France, just 14 miles (22km) across the water from the east coast, it is not surprising that Gallic dishes feature on menus. Firm favourites are *moules à la crème* (with Jersey cream, of course), *moules frites* or *plateau de fruits de mer*. But generally speaking it is British cuisine that prevails. You never have to go far to find a fry-up breakfast, Sunday roast, scampi and chips, or pots of tea that you can take down to the beach.

## WHERE TO EAT

For a tiny island Jersey has a remarkable number and variety of restaurants. You can choose from fashionable gastropubs, French restaurants, chic bistros, bustling trattorias, rustic inns and ethnic eateries. St Helier has the largest number of places to eat but Gorey and St Aubin both have highly rated restaurants, some with great views overlooking the sea. St Brelade's also has a good choice, from smart hotel dining to casual cafés virtually on the beach – a great spot for an early evening meal, watching the sun dip into the Atlantic.

Eating out at lunchtime, when many restaurants offer good-value two-course set menus, is often cheaper than evening dining. Hours are the same as those in the UK at lunchtime, but evening meals tend to be served earlier, especially at seaside restaurants where last orders are often at 8 or 8.30pm or even earlier. In summer it's usually wise to reserve a table in advance, especially if it's a warm evening and you want to dine alfresco.

## SHELLFISH

The clear, Gulf Stream-warmed waters around the island produce an abundance of shellfish including scallops, lobsters, chancre- or spider crabs, oysters and razor clams. The plump chancre crab

Fresh crab claws

is the most widely available but the sweeter spider crab is more sought after. Oysters, which used to thrive along the shores of the east coast, have seen a resurgence through farming at Grouville. Up to 600 tonnes of oysters are harvested here annually, making it the biggest production in the British Isles. The oyster seed is brought from hatcheries in France, then grown in netted sacks on the beach for around 18 months by which time they have reached their selling weight. Seventy percent are exported to the UK and France. The sweet and succulent 'Bouchot' mussels are also farmed on the coast here, grown from seed on wooden poles.

## ORMERS

If you happen to be on the beach from October to April during the neap tides, you might spot locals scouring the rocks at low tide in search of the near-mythical gastropod: the ormer. This indigenous mollusc, related to the abalone, is prized for its unique flavour and mother-of-pearl inner shell. The Channel Islands are the most northerly of its habitats and it was once a staple of island dinner tables. Traditionally the shellfish were carried home in a basket, soaked, shelled, scrubbed, beaten with a steak hammer, browned in a frying pan, then cooked in a casserole with belly of pork, shallots and carrots. Overfishing led to the ormer becoming a gourmet rarity, and nowadays there are stringent regulations to protect it. Fishing is only permitted between October and April, and only on the first day of each new or full moon and the five days following. Those who flout the rules are subject to hefty fines.

## FISH

Among the fish that still inhabit Jersey waters – and which are most commonly seen on menus – are sea bass, bream, brill, grey mullet, mackerel and sole. You'll also come across turbot, which is farmed in a German bunker on the east coast. The catch of the day is likely to vary daily and will probably be chalked up on a board. Local doesn't mean cheap, and if the fish is served by weight, check out what you're in for before giving the order. Jersey sea bass is becoming harder to find – a lot of what you see on menus is farmed in Spain, and it's not a patch on the line-caught bass fresh from Jersey waters.

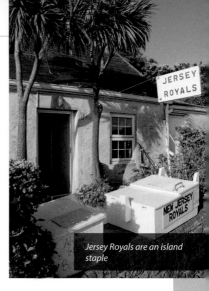
*Jersey Royals are an island staple*

## JERSEY ROYALS

First propagated in 1880 and traditionally fertilised by seaweed, Jersey Royal potatoes have earned worldwide acclaim not only for their waxy texture and earthy, nutty taste but the fact that they are ready well before the earliest crops of new potatoes in the UK. If you happen to be in Jersey in April, there is nothing to beat the very first crop of the season, straight from the soil, and served with Jersey butter and a sprinkling of parsley.

Jersey Royals are grown on the island's steeply sloping fields or *côtils*, and have never been grown outside the island. They are the only potato to be protected by a PDO (Protected Designation of Origin) under the Common Agricultural Policy of the European Union.

## JERSEY VEGETABLES

Fresh, locally produced fruit and vegetables include strawberries, asparagus, broccoli, courgettes, peppers, tomatoes, and shitake mushrooms. You will see some of the produce when you are travelling round the island. Honesty boxes are left at the roadside – you choose what you want and leave the correct change. Elsewhere, look for the Genuine Jersey Mark – the guarantee of local provenance. This applies to produce reared, grown and caught in Jersey, including dairy goods, fruit and vegetables, meat and poultry, fish, wines, ciders, spirits and beers. The island has around 15 'Genuine Jersey' farm shops.

## LOCAL SPECIALITIES

Before the days of Jersey Royals, red and white beans were the island staples. They were grown on every farm on the island and it was the Jersey beans that inspired the Heinz baked variety – or so it's said. The beans were an essential ingredient of the hearty, cassoulet-like Jersey Bean Crock, cooked with pigs' trotters, belly of

### THE JERSEY COW

Symbolic of the island, the Jersey cow is known for the richest milk in the world. The handsome tan and white doe-eyed cows feature as watermarks on Jersey bank notes – as well as on numerous souvenirs from milk jugs to tea towels. The purity of the breed has been guaranteed since 1789 when a ban was imposed on the import of live cattle to the island. Since the end of the 18th century it has been exported worldwide and there is still high demand. India, Japan, New Zealand, America and Fiji are just a few of the countries where the breed can be found. Jersey dairy products include butter, cream, yoghurt, organic milk, ice cream, crème fraîche and clotted cream, popular of course with Jersey cream teas. Those watching the waistline or cholesterol level can always opt for the fat-reduced or low-fat Jersey milk, which is widely available.

pork and onion and served with cabbage loaf, a delicious doughy gold-crusted bread baked in large cabbage leaves. The bread can still be found in some bakeries. Just occasionally you come across *des Mèrvelles*, or Jersey Wonders, which taste like doughnuts (without the jam) and are shaped in a figure of eight. Jersey housewives traditionally cooked them as the tide went out. They also cooked vraic buns, cakes made with yeast and raisins, and named after the vraic, or seaweed, which is collected from beaches and used as fertiliser. In days gone by families would gather to collect vraic from the beach, snacking on the buns (and swigging cider) between seaweed-collecting stints.

## Black Butter

The unappetisingly-named Jersey black butter, or *le nier beurre*, is not butter at all, but a type of apple preserve used to spread on bread or toast. Islanders made this in enormous quantities in

*A delicious cream tea*

the days when the cider industry was flourishing. Typically 700lb (318kg) of sliced apples, 20lb (9kg) of sugar, 24 lemons, spices and liquorice were added to a large copper urn with 10 gallons (45l) of cider. The pot was stirred day and night, amid song, dance and general merriment, then poured into jars to last until the next black butter-making session. The Jersey National Trust (www.national-trust.je) keeps the tradition alive, and if you happen to be in Jersey on the last weekend of October you can pitch in and help with peeling or stirring the pot in the bakehouse at The Elms, La Cheve Rue, St Mary. Black butter can be bought at La Mare Vineyards or from Maison La Mare, 33 King Street, St Helier.

## WINE AND CIDER

Jersey is pleasantly sunny, and shares the same degree of latitude as the Champagne region, so it's only natural the island should produce its own fizz. La Mare Wine Estate, St Mary, produces Cuvée de la Mar, a sparkling Brut wine made in the traditional *méthode champenoise*, the same method used in the Champagne region (after which is it named). Following the success of the Cuvée, La Mare is now producing a pink fizz called Lillie – after Jersey's Lillie Langtry. Still white and red wines, apple brandy, liqueurs and a delicious French-style sparkling cider are also made at La Mare.

Cider was first introduced to the Channel Islands by the Normans and until relatively recently it was the main drink of the island. In the 17th century it was given by farmers to their staff to make up their wages. At the cider festival at Hamptonne Country Life Museum in October, you can watch the old cider-making methods, with a horse crushing the apples and the juice extracted on the twin-screw press.

## CULINARY EVENTS

The island hosts a fast-growing number of foodie events, kicking off with the Spring Specials (mid-February to the end of March) when almost half the island's restaurants show off the best of their culinary skills and offer great-value set-price menus. Serious foodies should visit the island in late May during the week-long Food Festival, which celebrates the best from Jersey's food producers and chefs. The *Tennerfest* (six weeks from October to mid-November) is hugely popular; fixed price menus starting at £10 are on offer at 150 restaurants, including many of the best. At many fairs stalls sell everything from Jersey oysters to gourmet burgers. The Gorey *Fête de la Mer* in May is known for alfresco seafood dining; the *Foire de Jersey* features food stalls, French markets, and a Cheese Festival. October sees *Le Fais'sie d'Cidre* (Cider Festival), a lively event held at Hamptonne Country Life Museum to celebrate the island's heritage of apple cultivation and cider production.

# WHERE TO EAT

The price bands are based either on a two-course evening meal for one with a glass of house wine or for lunch where no evening meal is served. Prices exclude service charge, but are inclusive of the 5 percent Goods & Services Tax:

| | |
|---|---|
| ££££ | over £40 |
| £££ | £30–40 |
| ££ | £ 20–30 |
| £ | under £20 |

## ST HELIER

**Banjo ££–£££** *8 Beresford Street, tel: 01534 850890;* www.banjojersey.com. Converted from the Victoria Club, a private men's club next to the market, this is now part of the Jersey Pottery emporium. It comprises a stylish brasserie, a casual restaurant and an all-day café/bar, along with four chic guest rooms on the second floor. Closed all day Sunday and on Mondays during summer.

**Bohemia ££££** *Green Street, tel: 01534 880588;* www.bohemiajersey.com. One of Jersey's top gourmet restaurants within the chic contemporary surrounds of the Club Hotel and Spa. Chef Callum Graham produces dishes such as aged Jersey angus beef tartare with braised short rib or pan-fried mullet with courgette and coriander, red pepper, harissa, and pickled cockles. Daily noon–2.30pm & 6–10pm.

**Café Jac £** *Jersey Arts Centre, Phillips Street, tel: 01534 879482;* www.cafejac. co.uk. Popular, good value and friendly café where you can turn up for breakfast, brunch and light bites any time of day, and enjoy globally-inspired full meals. Good choice of vegetarian dishes, takeaways available, tables outside. Mon–Fri 7am–9pm, Sat 7.30am–4pm.

**Cock and Bottle ££** *Royal Square, tel: 01534 722 184;* www.liberationgroup. com. Traditional pub with alfresco dining on the square (heaters and blankets provided); perfect for a sunny day to enjoy mussels and fries or pub favourites, with chilled wine or a beer. Inside, original 18th-century features have been retained. Mon–Sat noon–4pm.

**The Fresh Fish Company ££** *Victoria Pier, tel: 01534 736799;* www.jersey.com/see-and-do/fresh-fish-company. Savour a crab sandwich or lobster claw with a sea view or select fish from the retail shop to grill on a beach BBQ. The company supplies many hotels and restaurants with local fish. Tues–Sat 8am–2pm, Sun 8am–1pm.

**The Green Olive ££–£££** *1 Anley Street, tel: 01534 728198;* www.greenoliverestaurant.co.uk. A popular bistro-style restaurant renowned for creating mouthwatering menus from local produce, *The Green Olive* specialises in fusion food using Mediterranean and Asian flavours. Tues–Thurs 6am–9.30pm, Fri–Sat 6am–10pm.

**The Lamplighter £** *9 Mulcaster Street, tel: 01534 723119.* The Lamplighter is renowned for its real ales, with four direct from the cask. This is a traditional town pub with wooden beams and working gas lamps, though not without its TV screens for watching the big games. Snacks and soup are served at scrubbed pine tables. Tues–Sun 11am–11pm.

**Samphire £££** *7-11 Don Street, tel: 01534 725100;* www.samphire.je. A Michelin-starred restaurant delivering consistently high-quality cuisine in a stylish but relaxed setting. It offers all day dining options, and has two terraces for alfresco meals or drinks. Tues–Fri 9am–late, Sat 10am–late.

**Thai Dicq Shack £** *Dicq Slipway, Dicq Road, St Saviour, tel: 1534 730273;* www.thaidicqshack.je. Bring your own bottle and chill on the sands with tasty, freshly cooked Thai cuisine. Try red snapper stir fry with lemon and ginger, Thai curry or plum and lemon ginger ribs. Daily 5–9pm.

**Tassili ££££** *Grand Jersey, The Esplanade, tel: 01534 722301;* http://www.handpickedhotels.co.uk/grandjersey/eat-drink. The opulent *Tassili* restaurant, located in the five-star Grand Jersey hotel, offers the ultimate in gourmet cuisine. Chef Nicolas Valmagna's menus are inspired by his French heritage and love for fresh Jersey produce, and feature a selection of local ingredients. You get what you pay for though, so go with well-lined pockets, and if you're really pushing the boat out try the chef's nine-course surprise menu – with a selection of his favourite dishes. Wed–Sat 6–8.30pm.

# AROUND THE ISLAND
## Bonne Nuit

**Bonne Nuit Beach Café £** *Bonne Nuit Beach, tel: 01534 861656*. This inviting beach café has lovely views of the fishing harbour. Come for full English breakfasts, light lunches, seafood specials, crab sandwiches and classic Thai dishes using fresh local ingredients. Takeaway also available. The cafe is not licensed so BYOB. Daily 8.30am–8.45pm.

## Gorey

**Bass and Lobster Foodhouse ££–£££** *Gorey Coast Road, tel: 01534 859590; www.bassandlobster.com*. Chef Dave Jones is well-known for championing Jersey produce, whether it's hand-dived scallops, chancre crab or line-caught sea bass. For variety try the tasting plate, which changes daily. Despite the name of the restaurant there is always a choice of meat on the menu – again, mainly locally sourced. Tues–Sat noon–2pm & 6–8.30pm, Sun noon–3pm.

**Crab Shack Gorey ££** *La Route de la Côte, tel: 01534 850830; www.jerseycrab-shack.com*. Part of Jersey Pottery, this is a popular Gorey eatery with great views of the castle and creative cuisine. Come for a light lunch or leisurely dinner and expect crab linguine, California-style crab tacos, sirloin steak, and Indonesian seafood curry. There is an unusually good choice of wines, many served by the glass. Tues–Sat noon–2pm & 6–9pm, Sun noon–2pm.

**Suma's £££** *Gorey Hill, tel: 01534 853291; www.sumasrestaurant.com*. The little sister of *Longueville Manor*, *Suma's* is a small, stylish restaurant serving innovative British cuisine with the emphasis on the best of Jersey's seafood. The dining room is bright and modern but the sought-after seats in summer are those on the terrace with outstanding views of Grouville Bay and Mont Orgueil Castle. Dishes are artfully presented and full of flavour. Choose from the *à la carte* or set menus. Wed–Sat 6–8.30pm, Thurs–Fri noon–2.30pm, Sat 11am–2.30pm, Sun noon–2.30pm.

## Grève de Lecq

**Moulin de Lecq ££** *tel: 01534 482818*. The tavern is an ancient water mill with a stream that flows into the sea; it retains original stone and wood features and the main bar is built around the watermill's cog wheels and gearing mechanisms. The restaurant serves full meals and you can eat in the garden in summer. Mon & Wed–Sat noon–11pm, Sun until 7pm.

## Rozel

**The Hungry Man £** *Rozel Bay, tel: 01534 863227*. This kiosk on the waterside is famous for its delicious crab sandwiches. You can sit at port-side tables with views of the bay, and walk along the pier for views of France on a clear day. Tues–Sun 9.30am–4pm.

## St Aubin

**Lazin Lizard ££** *Charing Cross, Mont Les Vaux, tel: 01534 747740*; www. lazinlizard.com**.** Buzzy little restaurant with tasty dishes such as crispy squid, Jamaican Jerk chicken, sticky ribs and steak with teriyaki prawns. The emphasis is on fusion Asian with plenty of vegetarian options. Very popular - be sure to book. Tues–Fri 5.30–11.30pm, Sat noon–2.30pm & 5.30–11.30pm.

**Lookout Beach Café £-££** *First Tower, Victoria Avenue, tel: 01534 616886*; www.thelookoutjersey.com. Between St Helier and St Aubin, with views across the bay, this café is a favourite among locals.  Come for full English breakfasts, brunch (eggs Florentine or Benedict), hand-made burgers, seafood platter or fish 'n' chips. Daily specials are served in summer, based on available fresh ingredients. Mon & Wed–Sat 9am–9pm, Sun until 8pm.

**Mark Jordan at the Beach £££** *La Plage, La Route de la Haule, St Peter, tel: 01534 780180*; www.markjordanatthebeach.com. A casual bistro on the beachside promenade offering high-quality, simply-cooked cuisine with an emphasis on fish. The retro desserts like sticky toffee pudding are hard to resist. Tues–Sun noon–2.30pm & 6–9.30pm. Closed Mon and Tues in winter.

**Salty Dog Bar and Bistro £££** *Le Boulevard, St Aubin's Village, tel: 01534 742760;* www.saltydogbistro.com. Stylish, laid-back eatery offering fusion cuisine, with food that is big on flavour, freshness and spice. A Thai spicy beef salad or pan-roasted seabass fillet might be followed by the sumptuous surf and turf (lobster, scallops and king prawns with prime beef fillet in a chilli, garlic and coriander sauce), then a 'Gooey Jersey Black Butter & Banana Toffee Pudding'. Cocktails and contemporary music are part of the scene. Wed–Sat noon–2.30pm & 6–9.30pm, Sun noon–3.30pm & 6–9.30pm.

## St Brelade's and Ouaisné Bay

**Crab Shack £–££** *St Brelade's Bay, tel: 01534 850855,* www.jerseycrab-shac.com. A casual, all-day eatery with a terrace right on the bay. There are fry-up breakfasts, fish and chips, BBQ ribs and Jersey chancre crab, which comes with a shell-cracking wooden mallet. Winter Tues–Thurs, Sun noon–2pm, Fri–Sat noon–2pm & 6–8pm; summer Wed–Sun noon–2pm & 6–8.30pm.

**Flavour Bay Cafe ££** *St Brelade's Bay, tel: 07829 996622.* Apart from a great location right on the island's most scenic beach, this café serves excellent seasonal food prepared using local produce. Particular highlights include filling Japanese ramen and delicious organic juices. It's very casual – you can turn up straight from the beach.

**Kismet Cabana £** *Ouaisné Bay, tel: 07700 809863;* www.kismetcabana.com. Street food inspired by global flavours. Come for all-day breakfasts, jerk curry, creative burgers and a good choice of vegetarian, vegan and gluten-free dishes. This laid-back shack is behind the car park but there is Beach Club seating on the bay. Winter Mon–Thurs 9am–3pm, Fri–Sat until 4pm; summer Sun–Thurs 9am–5pm, Fri & Sat 9am–8pm.

**Old Portelet Inn £–££** *Portelet, St Brelade, tel: 01534 741899;* www.randalls-jersey.co.uk/the-portelet-inn. This huge family pub in an old farmhouse has a bar, bistro and lovely views of Portelet Bay. Play areas inside and out, live entertainment most evenings, piped music. Mon–Thurs noon–2.30pm & 4.30–8pm, Fri–Sat until 8.30pm, Sun noon–7pm.

**Old Smugglers Inn ££** *Ouaisné Bay, tel: 01534 741510; www.oldsmugglersinn.com.* These converted 18th-century cottages have real ales, log fires and a good range of pub food. House specials include king prawns in sweet and sour sauce, lamb shanks and traditional fish & chips. Mon–Fri noon–2pm & 5.30–8.30pm, Sat noon–9pm, Sun noon–5pm.

**Oyster Box £££–££££** *St Brelade's Bay, tel: 01534 850888; www.oysterbox.co.uk.* A stylish restaurant right on the bay, where you can pop between ocean dips or beach games for a burger or gourmet sandwich, or linger over a sumptuous platter of *fruits de mer*. Excellent choice of seafood including crab taglierini, monkfish scampi and battered haddock. The setting is contemporary, with fish-themed decor and alfresco terrace tables. Like the neighbouring *Crab Shack*, this is part of the ever-expanding Jersey Pottery emporium. Summer Tues–Thurs noon–2.30pm & 6–8.30pm, Fri–Sat until 9pm, Sun noon–2.30pm; winter Wed–Sat noon–2pm & 6–8.30pm, Sun until 2.30pm.

**Pizza Express £–££** *St Brelade's Bay, tel: 01534 499049; www.pizzaexpress.com.* The pizzas here are enhanced by the panoramic views from the huge picture windows. A takeaway menu is available. Sun–Wed 11.30am–9.30pm, Thurs–Sat until 10pm.

**Portelet Bay Café ££** *Portelet Bay; tel: 01534 728550.* Family-run café right on the beach with quirky upcycled decor. Delicious wood-fired pizzas and the catch of the day, brought in by boat. A lovely scenic spot, worth the trek down (no car access). Open daily; booking is essential in summer.

## St Clement

**Green Island Restaurant £££** *Green Island, tel: 01534 857787; www.greenisland.je.* The southernmost restaurant in the UK, *Green Island* has great sea views and outstanding seafood. The terrace overlooks Green Island itself, whose sandy beaches draw hordes of beach lovers in summer. There is a casual beach café atmosphere and a long list of locally sourced seafood such as lobster, langoustines, scallops, crayfish or Mediterranean classics such as crispy grilled sardines in garlic and lime. Meat dishes are also available. Wed–Sat noon–7.30pm, Sun until 6pm.

## St Ouen's

**El Tico ££** *St Ouen's Bay, tel: 01534 482009;* www.elticojersey.com. This contemporary beach cantina has great views of the surfing beach from its terrace and picture windows. The menu caters for all tastes and ages: sticky barbecue ribs, vegetarian mezze, gourmet burger, crab linguine and Sri Lankan curry. It is open all day for surfers' breakfasts, coffee, teas and casual meals. Winter Mon–Sat 5–8.30pm, Sun 5.30–8.30pm; summer Mon–Sat 5–9pm, Sun 5.30–8.30pm.

**Koru Arms ££** *La Route de la Pulente, tel: 01534 744487.* At the southern end of St Ouen's, this is a friendly pub offering steaks, burgers and seafood. It's also a great spot to watch the sunset over the Five Mile Beach. Mon–Thurs 11am–10pm, Fri–Sat until 11pm.

**Le Braye £** *La Grande Route des Mielles, tel: 01534 481395;* www.lebraye.com. Gaze across the huge bay of St Ouen's and stoke up on a big breakfast before a dip in the Atlantic. Or come for crustaceans, Jersey beef veggie burgers or cream teas. This is one of the safer areas for swimming at St Ouen's so it's very popular with families. Summer Mon–Sat 9am–9pm, Sun 9am–9pm; shorter hours off season.

**Ocean Restaurant ££££** *Atlantic Hotel, Le Mont de la Pulente, tel: 01534 744101;* www.theatlantichotel.com. Dine in style in one of Jersey's top-end restaurants with breathtaking views over the gardens to St Ouen's Bay. The hotel restaurant is renowned for classic British cuisine with a modern twist – red wine marinated venison loin, roast guinea fowl breast, steamed Dover sole paupiette. Head chef Will Holland uses the finest and freshest from Jersey's coast and countryside. Open daily.

## St Saviour

**Longueville Manor ££££** *Longueville Road, tel: 01534 725501;* www.longuevillemanor.com. This country house hotel has a long-standing reputation for gastronomy. Meals are served in the elegant wood-panelled Oak Room or the bright and airy Garden Room. Cuisine is contemporary English/French, with the emphasis on Jersey ingredients. Impeccable service; fine wine list. Daily noon–2pm & 6.30–8pm.

# TRAVEL ESSENTIALS

## PRACTICAL INFORMATION

# A

## ACCOMMODATION

Hotel accommodation ranges from B&Bs, yurts and converted forts to country manor houses and luxury town hotels. Several of the top hotels have undergone multimillion-pound refurbishments, and over a quarter of the hotel guest rooms are now within the four- and five-star range. Budget hotels, however, are hard to come by. Self-catering is becoming more popular with the opening of new complexes with good facilities. The accommodation section of the official Jersey website (www.jersey.com/stay) is very useful for finding accommodation.

If you are going in July and August it is wise to book well in advance, especially if you require a room with a view. At other times of year there is little problem. Many hotels are closed from November to February. Most establishments will require a deposit or credit card details before confirming a reservation. A large number of hotels have special offers, such as three nights for the price of two or free car hire with three or more nights' stay. Booking online at some hotels can save you 10 percent.

Specialist travel agents for Jersey who can organise tailor-made holidays with travel, transfers, insurance and car hire, include JerseyTravel.com (tel: 01534 496650, www.jerseytravel.com) and Channel Islands Direct (tel: 0800 6409058, www.channelislandsdirect.co.uk). Condor Ferries (tel: 0345 6091026, www.condorferries.co.uk) can organise accommodation if you are taking a car across on a Condor Ferry from Poole or Portsmouth.

**Self-catering** specialists include Freedom Holidays (tel: 0800 2335259, www.freedomholidays.com) or Macoles Self Catering (tel: 01534 488100, www.macoles.com). For a holiday with a difference, you can stay at one of the beautifully sited fortresses, observation towers and follies that have been restored by Jersey Heritage (www.jerseyheritage.org) as self-catering accommodation. They include the red-and-white striped Archirondel Tower near St Catherine's Breakwater, the Barge Aground folly at St Ouen's, the German Radio Tower overlooking the Corbière Lighthouse, the Seymour Tower, La

Crête Fort and Fort Leicester, both on the North Coast and an apartment in Elizabeth Castle.

Many visitors base themselves in St Helier, which has a good bus service to all parts of the island and is the starting point for island bus and boat tours. However, some of the smaller centres such as St Aubin, Gorey or St Brelade's Bay are far more picturesque, and have some excellent restaurants and good transport links.

## AIRPORT

Jersey Airport (www.jerseyairport.com) is located in St Peter, 5 miles (8km) west of St Helier. Taxis are metered and cost from £15–£22 from the airport to St Helier, depending on the location of your hotel. Bus No. 15 operates roughly every 20 minutes in season to St Helier via Red Houses and St Aubin, taking about 30 minutes. Tickets can be bought on the bus.

# B

## BICYCLE HIRE

For the energetic and eco-friendly, there is a 96-mile (155km) network of well-marked cycle routes, including Green Lanes where the speed limit is 15mph (24kmph). A cycling guide and map can be picked up from the Jersey Tourism Visitor Centre in St Helier and their website (www.jersey.com) gives details of bike-hire locations and guided bike tours. In St Helier you can hire bikes from the locally-owned Zebra Hire (9 The Esplanade opposite the bus station, tel: 01534 736556). Their bikes can be collected at the airport, harbour or from their shop in town. Adult and child mountain bikes, electric bikes, tandems, touring bikes and trailers are all available.

Visitors coming to the island on Condor Ferries can bring bikes to the island free of charge.

## BUDGETING FOR YOUR TRIP

The cost of flights from the UK vary hugely, from around £90 to £350 return, depending on the airline, time of year and day of the week (weekends are invariably more expensive). Hotel accommodation ranges from £80 for a double room in a basic guesthouse, £150 in a 3-star hotel and £200–£400 in a luxury hotel. Restaurant prices are similar to those in the UK. A pint of beer or lager is £3.25–£3.50; a bottle of house wine £8–£20; soft drink £1.45, cup of coffee £2–3; cycle hire from £16 per day or £50 a week.

Most attractions are free for young children and substantial reductions are given to senior citizens and students.

# C

## CAMPING

The island has only three campsites and reservations are advisable. The latest addition is the cushy Durrell Wildlife Camp at Jersey Zoo (tel: 01534 860097, www. durrell.org/wildlife/visit/hospitality/camp), which provides spacious pods with carpets, king-size beds, wood-burning stoves and outdoor decks with sunbeds as well as showering and kitchen facilities. You wake to the sound of lemurs or the sight of gibbons or red squirrels in the trees by your tent. Cooking equipment is supplied and the zoo has two cafés. There are additional teepees for children if required. Campers are allowed unlimited access to the wildlife park any time during their stay. Minimum stay is normally three nights. Beuvelande (tel: 01534 853575, www.campingjersey.com) in St Martin is the biggest campsite, with excellent facilities; the family-run, good-value Rozel Camping Park (tel: 01534 855200, www.rozelcamping.je) has views of France from one of its four fields and is within walking distance of the pretty harbour of Rozel, renowned for good restaurants. Both sites have a heated swimming pool and are only open from mid-May to September. Camping off-site is against the law and it is forbidden to pitch a tent anywhere on the island except on a designated site.

## CAR HIRE

The minimum legal age to hire a car is 20 and there are varying maximum age restrictions. A valid driving licence is required, with no endorsements for dangerous or drunken driving in the last five years. Some companies impose an upper age limit. Car hire companies are plentiful and there is little difference in price between the international and local companies. A small car costs from £76 per day or from £209 a week. Hire firms include:

**Avis** (tel: 0800 735 1110, www.avisjersey.co.uk)
**Europcar** (tel: 0800 735 0 735, www.europcarjersey.com)
**Hertz Rent-A-Car** (tel: 01534 636666, www.hertzci.com)

All rented cars are branded with a large letter H on the number plate.

## CLIMATE AND TIDE

Jersey has the highest average number of sunshine hours in the British Isles, although the summer temperatures are no higher than those in some parts of southern England. In the summer months the island has a daily average of eight hours of sunshine and an average maximum temperature of 68°F (20°C). As in the UK, the best months to go are from May to September, the hottest months being July and August. High temperatures in mid-summer are tempered by sea breezes. The following chart gives the average maximum temperature for St Helier.

|     | J | F | M | A | M | J | J | A | S | O | N | D |
|-----|---|---|---|---|---|---|---|---|---|---|---|---|
| °C  | 9 | 8 | 11 | 13 | 16 | 19 | 21 | 21 | 19 | 16 | 12 | 10 |
| °F  | 48 | 46 | 52 | 55 | 61 | 66 | 70 | 70 | 66 | 61 | 54 | 50 |

The sea temperatures are refreshing for swimming, averaging 62.8°F (17.1°C) in summer. The island has one of the largest tidal movements in the world. During spring tides Jersey's surface area increases from 45 to 63 sq miles (72 to 100 sq km) and the vertical difference between high and low water can be as much as 40ft (12 metres).

## CLOTHING

The climate is similar to that of the southern part of the UK and the average temperature only a couple of degrees warmer, so take a couple of sweaters and waterproofs even in summer. Otherwise T-shirts and shorts/skirts should suffice, not forgetting a sunhat, sunglasses and sun cream – the sun's rays can be deceptively strong. Casual wear is accepted in all but top-end hotels and restaurants where more formal wear would be expected. Some of the St Helier nightclubs refuse entry to anyone in jeans and trainers. On beaches the law requires that people 'do not act in a manner reasonably likely to offend public decency'. Topless bathing is generally accepted, though not widespread, and baring all on the island is inappropriate. Shopping in a swimsuit in St Helier is best avoided, too.

## CRIME AND SAFETY

Jersey is a safe place for a holiday but it is worth taking all the usual precautions: always lock car doors and don't leave your valuables unattended. Dial 999 for police, fire, ambulance or coastal rescue services. Report a loss or theft to the police within 24 hours if an insurance claim is to be made.

# D

## DRIVING

Jersey has the highest ratio of cars to people of anywhere in Europe, and around 36 percent of car trips on the island are less than 2 miles (3km). St Helier is notorious for traffic jams. Elsewhere driving is relatively stress-free, but beware of the very narrow lanes in the countryside, many of which are used by tractors, cyclists and pedestrians. Given these narrow lanes and the maximum speed limit of 40 mph (64kmph) there is no point in bringing or hiring a high-performance car – although a remarkable number of islanders seem to own them. Despite its small size the island has more than 350 miles (563km) of paved roads. You may lose your way in the rural interior but it won't be for long. Signposting is reasonably good and you are never very far from a village or beach resort.

Visitors bringing their own car to Jersey on Condor Ferries (www.condorferries. co.uk) must have an insurance certificate or International Green Card, a vehicle registration document, valid driving licence or International Driving Permit.

**Rules of the Road.** Rules reflect those of the UK: driving is on the left; seat belts are compulsory for adult front seat passengers, children must wear belts or a suitable child/infant restraint in both front and rear seats; it is an offence to hold a mobile phone while driving. Fixed alcohol limits and road-side breath testing are similar to the UK. Penalties are severe, with up to a £2,000 fine or 6 months' imprisonment for the first offence plus unlimited driving licence disqualification.

The maximum speed limit on the island is 40 mph (64kmph), reduced to 30 mph (50 kmph) or 20 mph (32 kmph) in built-up areas and 15 mph (24 kmph) on Green Lanes where priority is given to pedestrians, horses and cyclists. Yellow lines across roads at intersections indicate 'Stop and give way'. A single yellow line along the length of the kerb means parking is prohibited day or night, and is liable to a fine. The 'Filter in Turn' system, whereby vehicles from each direction take it in turn to cross or join the traffic from other directions, is used at some of the main junctions. Traffic lights in Jersey change from red to green with no amber in between.

In the event of an accident or breakdown call the police (tel: 999) who will advise the best course of action.

**Parking.** Parking requires the pre-purchase of paycards. These are available from Jersey Tourist Information Centre, hire car companies, post offices, garages, shops, Condor Ferries or anywhere displaying the paycard logo (a blue P inside a red C), but annoyingly not in the actual car parks that you need them for – Sand Street is the only exception. The cards are available as individual units or in books of 10 and are required from Monday to Saturday 8am–5pm in car parks with the paycard logo and on-street parking in the red and yellow zones. The charge for parking 'on-street' is one unit per stay. You are allowed to stay for 20 minutes in the yellow zone, 60 minutes in the red. The cards are not required at the harbour, airport and waterfront car parks, where a pay-on-exit scheme is operated.

# E

# ELECTRICITY

The current is the same as that of the UK, 240 volts AC, with British-style three-pin sockets. Visitors from other European countries will need an adapter; those from the US also need a transformer.

## EMBASSIES AND HIGH COMMISSIONS

**Australia** Australian High Commission, Australia House, The Strand, London WC2B 4LA; tel: 020 7379 4334, www.uk.embassy.gov.au.

**Canada** Canada High Commission, Canada House, Trafalgar Square, London SW1Y 5BJ; tel: 020 7004 6000, www.canadainternational.gc.ca.

**New Zealand** New Zealand High Commission, New Zealand House, 80 Haymarket, London SW1Y 4TQ; tel: 020 7930 8422, www.mfat.govt.nz.

**Republic of Ireland** Irish Embassy, 17 Grosvenor Place, London SW1X 7HR; tel: 020 7235 2171, www.dfa.ie.

**South Africa** South African High Commission, South Africa House, Trafalgar Square, London WC2N 5DP; tel: 020 7451 7299, www.southafricahouseuk.uk.

**United States** American Embassy, 33 Nine Elms Lane, London SW11 7US (mailing post code) SW8 5DB (GPS postcode); tel: 020 7499 9000, https://uk.usembassy.gov.

## EMERGENCIES

In an emergency, dial 999 for police, fire, ambulance or sea rescue.

# G

## GETTING TO JERSEY

Jersey Tourism (tel: 01534 859000, www.jersey.com) provides comprehensive information on air and ferry services from the UK. Year-round package holidays, either by sea or air for short or longer breaks, can be arranged through British tour operators. Specialist operators include JerseyTravel.com (tel: 01534 496650, www.jerseytravel.com) and Channel Islands Direct (tel: 0800 640 9058, www.channelislandsdirect.co.uk). Alternatively most of the hotels, guesthouses and self-catering establishments on the island can arrange travel for you, as well as travel insurance and car rental if necessary.

**By Air.** A dozen scheduled airlines and numerous charter operators service the island from nearly 50 destinations across the British Isles and mainland Europe. From London airports alone there are up to 12 flights a day. Off season the number of flights is reduced, especially from regional airports. From the

UK the main low-cost operator is Easyjet (www.easyjet.com) which flies from from Gatwick, Luton and half a dozen regional airports. British Airways (www.britishairways.com) operate regular flights from Heathrow. The best prices are normally secured by booking well in advance on the internet and avoiding weekends and the busiest times of year. When booking with low-cost carriers watch out for all the hidden extras. Prices vary considerably according to the time of year. Cheapest fares are normally secured by booking well in advance through the airline website and by avoiding high season and weekends.

The airline Aurigny (www.aurigny.com) provides a channel-hopping service between Jersey, Alderney and Guernsey.

**By Sea.** The only ferry line from the UK to Jersey is Condor Ferries (tel: 0345-6091026, www.condorferries.co.uk) who operate fast, state-of-the-art ferries to Jersey from Poole from April to October. The service takes around three hours if you go on a ferry direct to Jersey, over four if it stops at Guernsey en route. The wave-piercing catamarans all take cars and provide comfortable seating, duty-free shops with some excellent deals, a bar and café, and a play area for children. Club-class seating is available, with reclining seats and complimentary refreshments. The open deck affords spectacular views of Jersey as you arrive. Crossings can be rough and in bad weather ferries are occasionally cancelled. Condor also operates a year-round (Mon–Sat) traditional Clipper ferry from Portsmouth which takes 8–11 hours depending on whether the ferry stops at Guernsey. The return crossing is overnight with the option of 1-, 2- 3- or 4-berth cabins and en suite facilities.

**Inter-Island Ferries and France.** Condor (see above) operates a high-speed car ferry service between St Malo and Jersey (2 hours 30 mins) and between Guernsey and Jersey. Manches Iles Express (tel: 01534 880756 from Jersey, 0825 131 050 from France www.manche-iles.com) links Jersey with Guernsey and Sark, and has services from St Helier to Granville and Carteret in Normandy.

# GUIDES AND TOURS

Tantivy Blue Coach Tours (tel: 01534 706706, www.tantivybluecoach.com) is a long-established, reasonably-priced coach and tour operator offering all-day or half-day tours. Jersey Bus Tours (www.jerseybustours.com) operate two different tours in vintage open-top buses, departing daily April to September from Liberation Square. Hopper tickets allow unlimited travel on both routes.

# H

## HEALTH AND MEDICAL CARE

Covid-19 requirements for vaccinations and tests need to be verified prior to arrival in Jersey; you can check the requirements online at www.gov.je/Health/Coronavirus/Travel.

Apart from treatment solely within Jersey's A&E department, visitors have to pay for medical services and treatment. This includes emergency hospital treatment (such as operations) not within A&E, repatriation, out-patient appointments, GP visits and prescriptions. Australia, Austria, France, Guernsey and Alderney, Iceland, New Zealand, Norway, Portugal, Sweden and the UK have reciprocal care agreements with Jersey which cover emergency hospital treatment; however, the agreement does not cover certain types of follow-on treatment or travel costs. Visitors are therefore advised to take out comprehensive health insurance or check that their existing policy covers travel to the island.

The General Hospital at Gloucester Street, St Helier, JE2 3QS (tel: 01534 622000) has a 24-hour emergency unit. The majority of GP surgeries provide a service for visitors. Jersey Tourism can provide a leaflet with the details of island surgeries. Medical prescriptions can be dispensed at any of the island pharmacies.

Tap water is perfectly safe to drink.

# L

## LANGUAGE

English is spoken throughout the island but has only been the official language since the 1960s. The island's tradition is French, and even today some French words are used by the court and legal professions. In St Helier and other parts of the island you will see some street names in French, occasionally with the contemporary English names alongside. On rare occasions you can overhear some of the older residents speaking in Jèrriais, the local patois based on Norman French. Until World War II this dialect was widely spoken, with true French used to conduct written business. Local societies are anxious to keep the historic dialect alive; there are occasional pieces in Jèrriais in the *Jersey Evening Post* and the language is taught in some schools.

## LGBTQ+ TRAVELLERS

Jersey only decriminalised homosexuality as recently as 1990, but today the general attitude of islanders towards LGBTQ+ visitors is not so different from that in the UK. Same-sex partnerships on the island have been recognised since 2012 and there is a small, friendly LGBTQ+ scene on the island.

# M

## MAPS

At Jersey Tourism you can pick up the free Island Visitor Map showing attractions, sports facilities and cycle routes. A map of St Helier is also included. Free maps are also available from the bus station and most hotels. Should you require something more detailed you can purchase Perry's Guide in booklet form, which details every little lane. If you are walking your way around the island you might consider the Ordnance Survey style Jersey Official Leisure Map.

## MEDIA

All English national newspapers and many foreign ones arrive in Jersey in the early morning, weather permitting. The *Jersey Evening Post*, the island's Monday to Saturday newspaper, gives you a good idea of Jersey life, especially politics and gossip, and has useful practical information including the times of the tides and what's going on in terms of events and festivals on the island.

The free monthly *What's On* brochure, which you can pick up on arrival, or from Jersey Tourism, is packed with information on attractions and activities, including guided walks, beaches, entertainment and eating out. All national UK TV and radio stations can be picked up in Jersey and the majority of hotels have satellite TV.

## MONEY

English sterling is freely accepted on the island, as are UK cheques and all major debit and credit cards. Jersey issues its own banknotes (including a £1 note) and coins, and these can only be used in the Channel Islands. You will often be given change in Jersey currency, but UK banks will exchange Jersey notes (not coins) for sterling. You can also do this at the bank at Jersey airport, although a £30 limit is placed on changing cash amounts of Jersey currency to English sterling.

ATMs are widespread throughout Jersey. For currency exchange, banks generally offer a much better rate than *bureaux de change*. A few shops accept euros.

## OPENING HOURS

**Banks.** Banks have similar opening hours to those in the UK, with some open on Saturday morning.

**Shops.** Normal opening times are Mon–Sat 9am–5.30pm. There is no general Sunday opening in Jersey but the shops at Liberty Wharf, St Helier, and a few convenience food stores remain open. The markets and some shops are closed on Thursday afternoon.

**Tourist Attractions.** Most museums and tourist attractions are open from April to October; some are also open March to November, daily 10am–5pm, though the times are subject to change. Jersey Tourism can provide a list of current opening hours, or you can telephone them to check times for specific sites.

**Pubs.** Most pubs are open Mon–Sat 9am–11pm, Sun 11am–11pm.

# P

## POLICE

In an emergency dial 999. The police headquarters are at La Route du Fort, St Helier, JE2 4HQ (tel: 01534 612612). Along with the regular police Jersey has a network of honorary police officers who don't wear uniform.

## POST OFFICES

The main post office is in Broad Street, St Helier and is open Mon and Wed–Fri 8.30am–5 pm, Tue 9am–5pm, Sat 8.30am–1pm. Sub-post offices can be found throughout the island some with shorter opening hours. The island Bailiwick of Jersey has its own postal system and issues its own Jersey stamps, available from post offices and some shops. These must be used on all mail. Unlike the UK, mail is not divided into first and second class, there is just the one class. Jersey stamps are much in demand by collectors worldwide. The main post office has a philatelic display and stamp sales.

## PUBLIC HOLIDAYS

Jersey has the same public holidays as the UK with an additional day's holiday on 9 May, Liberation Day, commemorating the end of the German Occupation in 1945.

**1 January** New Year's Day
**March or April** Good Friday and Easter Monday
**First and last Mon in May** Spring Bank Holidays
**9 May** Liberation Day
**Last Monday in August** August Bank Holiday
**25 December** Christmas Day
**26 December** Boxing Day

## PUBLIC TRANSPORT

**Bus.** Jersey has an efficient, easy-to-use network of buses, operated by LibertyBus (tel: 01534 828555, www.libertybus.je). All buses radiate from the Liberation Station, St Helier. Bus timetables, with a map of the routes and a Liberation Station layout plan, are available online or free from the bus station; alternatively you can access them through WAP-enabled mobiles. For details go to the LibertyBus website. You can also text the bus stop code (shown beside the bus stop) to 07797 798888 to find out the arrival time of the next bus. A Hop-On Hop-Off ticket allows unlimited travel for 1, 2, 3 or 7 days and is available from the bus station. Summer services from mid-May until early October are far more frequent than those off season. Tickets can be purchased on the bus and are limited to one journey.

**Taxi.** Taxi ranks are only to be found at the airport, the arrivals building at the harbour and in various locations in St Helier. Rates vary according to the time and the day. Extra charges are made for waiting time and luggage carried in the boot. If you need a taxi call Citicabs, tel: 01534 499999, Liberty Cabs, tel: 01534 767700 or Yellow Cabs, tel: 01534 888888.

For a lift with a difference try LimoBikes (tel: 07797 749777,) who will pick you up on a Harley Davidson. Tours are also available.

**Le Petit Train.** The little tourist trains departing hourly with on-board commentaries are fun for families. They operate daily from April to October, between Liberation Square, St Helier and St Aubin. You can also board the train in West Port.

# R

# RELIGION

The established church in Jersey is the Church of England but Methodism has had a strong influence on many of the islanders since John Wesley preached here in 1787. Of the 29 Methodist chapels that existed here in the 19th century, 18 are still in use. There is also a notable Roman Catholic presence, with a total of eight churches. Jersey Tourism Centre publishes a leaflet with the times and places of services for various faiths and denominations.

# T

# TELEPHONE

The UK telephone code for Jersey is 01534. When dialling from outside the UK preface the code by 44 (for the UK) and omit the 0. STD codes for the UK from Jersey are the same as those used from the UK. As in the UK, international calls can be dialled direct from any public phone.

**Mobile Phones.** Beware that Jersey does not work on the UK system and there can be high charges for making and receiving calls on a UK mobile. Prices are set by the relevant UK service provider and, as the UK networks do not extend to Jersey, these are usually costed as international calls. The three Jersey networks are JT Jersey/Guernsey – which has the best coverage, Airtel-Vodafone and Sure. The network extends to the other Channel Islands. Visitors with mobiles will either be linked automatically to a network or can select the network manually.

Some pay as you go phones do not function in Jersey so check with your provider before you go.

## TIME ZONES
As in the rest of the UK, the Channel Islands are on Greenwich Mean Time (GMT), with clocks moving forward in late March, and reverting back in late October.

| New York | **Jersey** | Paris | Jo'burg | Sydney | Auckland |
|----------|------------|-------|---------|--------|----------|
| 7am | **noon** | 1pm | 2pm | 11pm | 1am |

## TIPPING
Tip as you would in the UK. In restaurants service is often added to the bill, in which case there is no need to tip.

## TOILETS
There are clean public toilets at main sites and at most beaches. Cafés are usually laid back about the public using their facilities, although if you buy a drink it will be appreciated.

## TOURIST INFORMATION

The Jersey Tourist Information Centre (tel: 01534 859000, www.jersey.com) is located within the bus station (Liberty Station) at 17 Esplanade, St Helier. The office has free maps and can arrange accommodation as well as provide tourist information on the island. It is open all year, daily 9am–5pm.

The monthly magazine *What's On*, which can also be picked up at the airport or harbour on arrival, contains a complete listing of events, and has information on attractions, activities, sports and entertainment. The Visitor Map of Jersey, available from Jersey Tourism Visitor Centre, marks all the main attractions of the island, along with sporting facilities and cycle routes. It includes a useful map of St Helier showing accommodation and town attractions.

## TRAVELLERS WITH DISABILITIES

For detailed information covering accommodation, transport, parking, attractions and equipment for hire for the disabled, visit www.jersey.com/accessible-tourism-visitor-guide. The local Citizens Advice Bureau (www.cab.org.je) also has information on Jersey for the disabled. Specialist organisations which can assist with holidays include Enable Holidays (www.enableholidays.com/Jersey). On-street parking and public car parks have designated areas for UK and European Blue Badge holders. A shopmobility service operates from St Helier's Sand Street Car Park from Mon–Sat 10am–4.30pm, also at Jersey Zoo and Jersey War Tunnels (information at www.shopmobility.org.je). The Radar National Key Scheme operates in Jersey, and toilets with radar locks can be found in main centres and at most beaches. Visitors are advised to bring their own key, but they are available for loan (£5 deposit required) from Jersey Tourism. Special wheelchairs designed for beach access are available from the charity Beachability (www.beachability.org, tel: 07797 935088).

# V

## VISAS AND ENTRY REQUIREMENTS

Jersey has the same passport and visa requirements as the UK. Although a passport is therefore not necessary for visitors arriving from the UK, airline passengers will need valid photographic ID in order to travel, and a passport is required for trips to France. Other EU citizens require passports.

Certain nationalities require visas regardless of the purpose of their stay in Jersey. The Jersey visa requirements are aligned to the UK visa requirements; you can check visa requirements on the GOV UK website at www.gov.uk/check-uk-visa. Schengen visas are not valid in Jersey.

As Jersey is not a full member of the European Union, you can still purchase duty-free items when travelling to and from the island. Maximum allowances are: 200 cigarettes or 250gr of other tobacco products; 1 litre of spirits or 4 litres of sparkling or fortified wines and 4 litres of other wines; 16 litres of beer or cider; 60cc/ml perfume; 250 cc/ml eau de toilette; £390-worth of other goods (watches, jewellery, cameras, etc).

# W

## WEBSITES AND INTERNET ACCESS

Wi-fi access is available at the airport, Jersey harbour lounge, Liberation bus station and most hotels and cafés. Most of the internet cafés are concentrated in St Helier. Free internet access and Wi-fi is available if you are eating or drinking at the Café Bar at the Pomme D'Or Hotel, Liberation Square, open Mon–Sun 7am–11pm. Jersey Library at Halkett Place offers free internet access and Wi-fi.

Here are some popular websites:

**www.jersey.com** The official Jersey website is packed with information and should cover all your needs, from how to get there, where to stay and eat, to transport, sports, activities and events. It is easy to use and gives interesting background information as well as all the practical details.

**www.islandlife.org** This is the largest community website serving the Channel Islands.

**www.jerseyeveningpost.com** The local paper with the latest Jersey news, weather, what's on and tides

**www.jerseyheritage.org** Details of all the Jersey Heritage sites to visit on the island and information on holiday lets in some of their quirky historic properties.

**www.libertybus.je** Everything you need to know about the Jersey buses.

**www.jerseyheritage.org** Information on many of the island's top attractions and a series of events from May to October, bringing to life the island's history.

**www.nationaltrust.je** Jersey's National Trust. If you are a member of the UK National Trust make sure you take your card when you go to Jersey. The Trust is the largest private land owner on Jersey, and is dedicated to preserving sites of historic, aesthetic and natural interest. Admission is free for NT members on production of a membership card. The organisation has a year-round programme of guided walks and events.

# Y

## YOUTH HOSTELS

Jersey's only YHA hostel has a unique setting in Jersey Zoo. In a traditional farmhouse, the hostel is often used by conservation experts and students who train at Durrell and by staying here you are making a contribution towards the Trust's work in helping save species from extinction. Prices start from £50 for Bed and Breakfast and include free entrance to the wildlife park. For more information visit www.durrell.org. (See also the newly-opened Durrell Wildlife Camp, page 116).

# WHERE TO STAY

The official Jersey Tourism website has a comprehensive illustrated guide to accommodation on the island, available at www.jersey.com/stay. For rooms in July and August book well ahead. Prices plummet in winter and you can get some great rates for weekends, Christmas and Easter, especially at the up-market hotels. Supplements are nearly always charged for sea-view rooms. Check the cost – it's often worth a little extra per night for the fabulous view you could wake up to.

The self-catering scene has improved with more seaside accommodation to rent, and, for the adventurous, the opportunity to stay in beautifully-located historic monuments and follies which have been restored by Jersey Heritage (tel: 01534 633300, www.jerseyheritage.org see page 114).

Grading of accommodation is optional but most establishments are assessed by the AA or VisitBritain (to the same criteria). Hotels, guesthouses and self-catering are assigned one to five stars, campsites one to five pennants. The rating reflects the overall quality of the experience, including hospitality, service, cleanliness and comfort; ie it is not based merely on facilities.

The price bands below are a rough indication of what you can expect to pay in high season (July–August) for a hotel double room with bathroom, including breakfast. Half-board rates usually offer better value than B&B rates.

| | |
|---|---|
| ££££ | over £220 |
| £££ | £180–220 |
| ££ | £130–180 |
| £ | under £130 |

## ST HELIER

**La Bonne Vie £** *Roseville Street, St Helier, tel: 01534 741305.* Charming Victorian guesthouse with a homely atmosphere, and flowers everywhere. The house was built for a wealthy merchant in the 1890s, and is located a few minutes' walk from the town centre, and just two minutes' from the beach where the Havre des Pas tidal pool guarantees bathing at all times. Guest rooms are individually furnished, some with handmade French four-poster beds.

**Club Hotel & Spa £££–££££** *Green Street, St Helier, tel: 01534 876500,* www. theclubjersey.com. Small and sophisticated, this luxury boutique hotel offers eight suites, 38 luxury rooms (complete with Bang & Olufsen portable telephones, feather beds and Frette Egyptian linen), a stylish spa with salt pool, thermal and *rasul* treatments and the gourmet *Bohemia* restaurant (see page 106).

**Elizabeth Castle Apartment ££££** *Elizabeth Castle, St Helier, tel: 0800 233 5259,* www.freedomholidays.com. Self-caterers with a sense of adventure will enjoy staying at the famous fortress in St Aubin's Bay. This is a small apartment (sleeps 4–6), set on two floors in the old barrack block off the parade ground. The setting is an islet, and when the sightseers leave the castle in the early evening you have the whole place to yourselves. The castle is only accessible by foot at low tide, but during castle opening hours an amphibious ferry operates every half hour at all tides.

**Grand Jersey Hotel & Spa ££££** *The Esplanade, St Helier, tel: 01534 722301,* www.handpickedhotels.co.uk. The revamped five-star Grand Jersey is swish and glamorous. You can sip vintage bubbles in the Champagne Lounge (with a choice of 35 champagnes and fine sea views), dine in the seductive *Tassili* restaurant, with its black backdrop, wind down or work out in the stylish Elemis spa and pool, or watch movies in the island's only private cinema.

**Monterey Hotel ££** *St Saviour's Road, tel: 01534 873006,* www.morvanhotels. com. Just a 10-minute walk from the centre of town, the Monterey offers comfortable modern accommodation and excellent leisure facilities. Main features include indoor and outdoor pools, spa bath, steam room and mini-gym.

**Royal Yacht ££££** *The Weighbridge, St Helier, tel: 01534 720511,* www.theroyalyacht.com. This revamped 1930s hotel has a state-of-the-art spa with pool, fully equipped gym, all-day grill restaurant and three bars, including a live music venue and champagne bar. For the ultimate in luxury opt for a penthouse suite, with a Jacuzzi on the harbour-view terrace and space for 10 guests to dine.

# AROUND THE ISLAND
## Gorey

**The Moorings ££** *Gorey Pier, St Martin, tel: 01534 853633,* www.themooringshotel.com. In the heart of Gorey, this small hotel sits at the foot of the ancient castle of Mont Orgueil. Many of the 15 rooms have views over the picturesque harbour, where boats depart for trips to Normandy. The restaurant is well known for Jersey specialities, especially the seafood platter.

## Grouville

**Beausite ££** *La rue des Pres, Grouville Bay, Grouville, tel: 01534 857577,* www.beausitejersey.com. Near Grouville beach, this was converted from a 17th-century granite farm building, with modern accommodation added. It is popular with families offering competitive rates for children. The leisure centre has a heated indoor pool, sauna, spa bath and a small gym. Self-catering accommodation is also available.

## Rozel

**Château La Chaire ££££** *Rozel Bay, St Martin, tel: 01534 863354,* www.chateau-la-chaire.co.uk. In a secluded spot at the foot of Rozel Valley, this Grade II listed country house hotel has a rococo lounge with fine mouldings, an oak-panelled dining room, a conservatory for lunches and 14 luxury rooms, some with spa bath and four-poster beds. The green valley stretches down to the delightful fishing creek of Rozel.

## St Aubin

**Harbour View ££** *St Aubin Harbour, tel: 01534 741585,* www.harbourview.je. Right in the centre of St Aubin, this creeper-clad guesthouse is set back from the road and picturesque harbour. Friendly, laid-back and family-run, it is one of Jersey's most popular guesthouses. There are 14 bedrooms, two suites and a welcoming garden terrace serving teas and light snacks.

**Hotel Cristina £££** *Mont Felard, St Aubin's Bay, tel: 01534 758024,* www.cristinajersey.com. Spectacular views of St Aubin's Bay are the main attraction of this refurbished hotel, and it's certainly worth paying the extra to secure a room with a south-facing balcony and sea view. Guests can dine at the brasserie-style Indigo restaurant, or have light refreshments in the lounge, terrace bar or around the pool.

**Millbrook House £** *Rue de Trachy, Millbrook, tel: 01534 733 036,* www.jersey.co.uk/hotels/millbrookhouse. This is a peaceful retreat, surrounded by 10 acres (4 hectares) of park and gardens, halfway between St Helier and St Aubin. Traditional decor, discreet service and very reasonable prices.

**Old Court House Inn ££** *St Aubin Harbour, tel: 01534 746433,* www.liberationgroup.com. This harbour-view hotel dates back to 1450 and in the 17th century the cellars were used to store the plunder of Jersey privateers. Guest rooms are individually furnished and include a two-bedroomed penthouse suite with a private sun terrace. Various eating areas include the cellar restaurant, floral courtyard to the rear and the deck over the harbour. Older visitors who remember Bergerac may recognise the inn – it was the *Royal Barge* in the popular 1980s TV series.

**The Panorama ££** *La Rue du Crocquet, tel: 01534 742429,* www.panoramajersey.com. This award-winning, welcoming B&B has fine bay views from picture windows, luxury beds with pocket springs and excellent breakfasts. Tea in the garden is a real treat, and for dinner there are plenty of good restaurants in the centre of St Aubin within easy walking distance. Non-smoking, adults only (no children under 18) and minimum stays of three or six nights depending on the time of year.

## St Brelade

**Atlantic Hotel ££££** *Le Mont de la Pulente, St Brelade, tel: 01534 744101,* www.theatlantichotel.com. This small and very desirable hotel, with dramatic views over the Atlantic, has been under local family ownership since it opened in 1970. It looks crisp, clean, light and contemporary. The striking sea-view *Ocean* restaurant, all in white, blue and beige, provides the backdrop for the exceptional cuisine, based on local ingredients (see page 112). Facilities include the Palm Club with indoor pool, spa pool, mini-gym and saunas, and an all-weather tennis court. The hotel backs on to La Moye Golf Club.

**Golden Sands Hotel £** *La Route de la Baie, tel: 01534 741241,* www.golden-sandsjersey.com. This hotel situated on a promenade has comfortable rooms overlooking the sea. The proximity of the sandy seashore makes the hotel a perfect location, especially for families with children. The restaurant's menu is extensive, and hotel guests can enjoy a cocktail, coffee or a snack on the veranda of the snug Café Bar.

**Les Ormes Self Catering ££££** *Mont à la Brune, St Brelade, tel: 01534 497000;* www.lesormesjersey.co.uk. Contemporary and well-equipped self-catering resort comprising Les Ormes leisure village near St Brelade's Bay and Les Ormes de la Mer coastal cottages, overlooking St Ouen's Bay. Accommodation comes with well-equipped kitchens and pocket-sprung king-size beds. *Les Ormes* offers a host of activities including an indoor (and seasonal outdoor) pool, gym, indoor tennis, nine-hole golf course and fun zone; *Les Ormes de la Mer* has great surf and stunning sunsets (and the use of the other Les Ormes facilities).(see page 95)

**L'Horizon Hotel & Spa ££££** *St Brelade's Bay, tel: 01534 743101,* www.hand-pickedhotels.co.uk. A house was originally built here in 1850 by a colonel in the Bengal Army – though he wouldn't recognise it now. *L'Horizon* has moved with the times. The interior is all space, light and elegance, the guest rooms contemporary in style with DVD players, free Wi-fi and MP3 docking stations, but the views haven't changed. Sitting right on one of the island's finest beaches, the hotel enjoys glorious sea views. In the unlikely event that the sea doesn't tempt you there is always the indoor saltwater spa pool, which has sea views.

**St Brelade's Bay Hotel ££££** *St Brelade's Bay, tel: 01534 746141,* www.stbreladesbayhotel.com. This comfortable, relaxing hotel, set in immaculate 7-acre (3-hectare) gardens and overlooking the best family beach on the island, is a winner. After five generations in the same family it has changed hands and been entirely refurbished in contemporary style and equipped with a state-of-the-art health club and a 20m swimming pool.

**Windmills Hotel ££** *Mont Gras d'Eau, St Brelade, tel: 01534 744 201*. Long-established, family-run hotel set on the hillside, with fine views of St Brelade's and Ouaisn Bay. Spacious terrace gardens, outdoor heated pool, sauna and mini-gym. Self-catering apartments are also available.

## St Clements

**Pontac House Hotel £** *La Grande Route De La Cote St Clement, tel: 01534 857771*, www.pontachouse.com. This intimate hotel for 55 guests is run by the Pinto family. The hotel has a swimming pool, offering an alternative for visitors if the tide is too high to swim in the sea. Free parking for guests makes this place a good starting point to set off for a road trip around the island

## St Peter

**Boscobel Country Apartments ££££** *Rue Des Vignes, St Peter, tel: 08000 124462*, www.boscobel.co.uk. Seven purpose-built apartments are set on an old Jersey farm, surrounded by extensive pastureland. Accommodation is traditional in style and well-equipped with satellite TV and high-speed broadband in every apartment, plus gardens and play area.

**Greenhills Country Hotel £££** *St Peter's Valley, St Peter, tel: 0845 8005555*, www.seymourhotels.com. A welcoming country house in the heart of St Peter's parish, *Greenhills* was converted from a late 17th-century home and still retains features from the original building. The 33 guest rooms combine country home elegance with modern comforts. The heated swimming pool is set in award-winning gardens.

## St Saviour

**Longueville Manor ££££** *Longueville Road, St Saviour, tel: 01534 725501*, www.longuevillemanor.com. The Channel Islands' most highly acclaimed hotel, this 14th-century manor is set in 15 acres (6 hectares) of fine gardens and woodland. No expense has been spared in the decor, with its elegant fabrics and fine antiques. The service is impeccable and the restaurant is renowned for fine cuisine – with vegetables fresh from the kitchen garden. To help work off the calories there is an all-weather tennis court and a heated outdoor pool.

**Merton Hotel ££** *Belvedere Hill, St Saviour, tel: 01534 724231,* www.seymourhotels.com/merton-hotel. A children's paradise, this resort hotel is best known for the aquatic thrills of the Aquadome. This domed indoor pool has water slides, cascade fountains, spa pools and the Flowrider artificial wave, the easy way to learn surfing and bodyboarding. Bedrooms are modern and functional, with good-value weekly rates.

## Trinity

**Durrell Wildlife Camp ££** *Les Augrès Manor, La Profonde Rue, Trinity, tel: 01534 860097,* www.durrell.org/wildlife/visit/hospitality/camp. For something completely different experience the luxury camp at Jersey Zoo, surrounded by rare animals. Accommodation is comfy yurts with carpets, proper beds, wood-burning stoves, safes and private bathrooms in separate tents. Cooking equipment is supplied and the zoo has two cafés. Guests have free access to the park. Minimum stay is normally three nights.

**Undercliff Guest House £-££** *Bouley Bay, tel: 0800 112 3058,* www.undercliffjersey.com. This is an ideal base for walkers, just 20 yds/m from the spectacular north coast footpath. Bouley's pebble beach, with its clear waters, is down the road. There are 13 self-catering, individually-styled rooms, as well as junior suites. The rooms are not serviced but have free continental breakfast supplies daily. The garden has a heated pool. Jersey Zoo is nearby and there is a bus service to St Helier in season.

# INDEX

# THE **MINI** ROUGH GUIDE TO
# JERSEY

**First Edition 2022**

**Editor:** Annie Warren
**Author:** Susie Boulton
**Updater:** Anita Chmielewska
**Picture Editor:** Tom Smyth
**Cartography Update:** Carte
**Layout:** Pradeep Thapliyal
**Head of DTP and Pre-Press:** Katie Bennett
**Head of Publishing:** Kate Drynan
**Photography Credits:** Andy Le Gresley
Photography/Seymour Hotels 6T; Corbis
21; iStock 7B; Mary Evans Picture Library 19;
Mockford & Bonetti/Apa Publications 4TC, 4MC,
4MC, 4TC, 4TL, 4ML, 5M, 6B, 7T, 11, 13, 18, 22,
26, 29, 31, 32, 33, 35, 37, 39, 40, 41, 42, 43, 44, 46,
47, 48, 50, 52, 54, 55, 56, 57, 60, 63, 64, 66, 68, 70,
71, 73, 74, 76, 77, 79, 80, 82, 84, 87, 88, 91, 93,
94, 99, 101, 103, 104; Shutterstock 1, 4ML, 5T,
5M, 16, 38, 96
**Cover Credits:** St Ouens Bay **Alagz/
Shutterstock**

**Distribution**
**UK, Ireland and Europe:** Apa Publications (UK)
Ltd; sales@roughguides.com
**United States and Canada:** Ingram Publisher
Services; ips@ingramcontent.com
**Australia and New Zealand:** Booktopia;
retailer@booktopia.com.au
**Worldwide:** Apa Publications (UK) Ltd;
sales@roughguides.com

**Special Sales, Content Licensing
and CoPublishing**
Rough Guides can be purchased in bulk
quantities at discounted prices. We can create
special editions, personalised jackets and
corporate imprints tailored to your needs. sales@
roughguides.com; http://roughguides.com

Printed in Poland

**Contact us**
Every effort has been made to provide accurate
information in this publication, but changes
are inevitable. The publisher cannot be held
responsible for any resulting loss, inconvenience
or injury sustained by any traveller as a result
of information or advice contained in the
guide. We would appreciate it if readers would
call our attention to any errors or outdated
information, or if you feel we've left something
out. Please send your comments with the
subject line "Rough Guide Mini Jersey Update" to
mail@uk.roughguides.com.